A
GOLDEN
STRING

DAISY NEWMAN

1817

HARPER & ROW, PUBLISHERS, SAN FRANCISCO

Cambridge, Hagerstown, New York, Philadelphia, Washington
London, Mexico City, São Paulo, Singapore, Sydney

FIRST EDITION

Library of Congress Cataloging-in-Publication Data

Newman, Daisy.
    A golden string.

    1. Newman, Daisy—Biography.
    2. Novelists, American—20th century—Biography.
    3. Fiction—Authorship.   I. Title.
PS3527.E877Z464   1987   813'.52 [B]   86-45820
ISBN 0-06-066105-4

for

Ruth Hapgood · Gordon and Edith Browne · Thomas and Katherine Perry

I give you the end of a golden string,
Only wind it into a ball,
It will lead you in at Heaven's gate . . .

William Blake, "Jerusalem III"

Foreword

Well, now that I've arrived at the age of maturity! Arrived, that is, if, in the coming years, I approximate the experience of my friend Sue.

"I really didn't grow up till I was in my eighties," she observed, shortly before her ninety-ninth birthday.

A giggle escaped me. Sue must always have been as wise as she was lovable.

Her eyes reproved me for not taking her seriously. "Then I began to do some thinking," she insisted.

On Sue's hundredth birthday, I recollected her paradoxical remark, regretting that I had betrayed amusement. She had clearly been trying to tell me something important.

Now I think I understand what she meant. Age does bring some heightening of awareness. Will I be given this insight in my eighties?

My *eighties?* Impossible!

I have to admit that the immediate effect was not one of sobering maturity but of recklessness. I no longer needed to save for my old age. It had arrived. I could splurge. And I could say anything I pleased. If it happened to be outrageous, it would be excused on the grounds of senility. I felt lighthearted, liberated.

For seven years I had been living in Lincoln, Massachusetts. Leaving my home in Hamden, Connecticut, where, for forty years, I had known so much joy and such deep sorrow, had been a wrench. But when I turned seventy it became clear that in my old age I ought to be living nearer one of my children. Cleveland, where Ellen and Irv, my daughter and son-in-law live, is, apart from their home, unfamiliar. In the Boston area, where Nicky and Kathy, my son and daughter-in-law live, I have roots. I studied and worked in Cambridge. Many of my friends are there. I've never regretted the move.

That this new decade would bring other changes—curtailment of activity, loss of independence, deterioration—I vaguely foresaw.

Still, I thought, if I'm fortunate, I too may be blessed with the late flowering Sue described. What a magnificent prospect!

The celebrations began weeks before my birthday in Greensboro, North Carolina, where the First Friends Meeting had invited me to be the "Visiting Friend." My old friends Floyd and Lucretia, with whom I stayed, initiated the festivities.

After I returned home, there was a surprise luncheon at my friend Bar's house in Weston, Massachusetts. Kathy had told me that she and her mother were taking me out to lunch. I suspected nothing. We drove to Bar's, where a dozen of my cherished friends were assembled: some verging on old age, the three young Quaker writers who meet at my house from time to time, two-year-old Hope, her father, and baby sisters.

The following evening, at the Monthly Meeting of Friends in Cambridge, the clerk presented me with a bouquet of daisies. They were, I learned later, a last-minute substitution for the balloons my playful friend Molly had intended to bring to the meetinghouse. Alas, she came down with flu. The flowers were much more sedate. I felt deeply honored.

Just the same, I wish Molly could have brought the

balloons into the meetinghouse. They would have touched the high ceiling with reverence; they would have given it the kiss of peace.

I can already predict that some day they'll appear in the little Kendal Friends Meetinghouse—that dear, imaginary place, where the characters in my novels find insight. A bevy of balloons, bright with celestial aspiration, will bob joyfully amongst the old rafters, as the breeze from Little Narragansett Bay blows gently through the windows.

Won't my characters—Serenity and Peter, Oliver and Loveday, and especially Ross and little Daphne—love that!

The festivities reached a climax when, surrounded by my entire family—Ellen and Irv, Nicky and Kathy, and the grandchildren, Jim, Nancy, and Carol—I listened to the concert, which was Nancy's present.

First she played a Bach suite for unaccompanied cello, transposed for the viola. Then she and Ellen played Mozart's Sinfonia Concertante for violin and viola, accompanied by a friend, while Carol turned the pages. Nicky taped the concert. I'll enjoy it as long as I can hear.

The music was so beautiful, the love with which it was offered so touching that I couldn't quite hold back the tears. I recalled the Mozart duet Ellen and Nancy played at the back of the Framingham Friends Meetinghouse seven years earlier, as George and I were about to enter and, in the presence of God and our friends, take each other in marriage.

I longed for George. We'd only been given such a short time together. But the children and grandchildren were upholding me.

Now the celebrations are over. What shall I write next? Unknown readers send me the most moving letters, asking for one more Kendal novel. My characters have become their friends.

I'd like to spend some time in Kendal myself.

Life goes on there, just as it does everywhere else. A year ago, Peter and Serenity had a little girl. They named her Daphne Otis Holland. She doesn't have Serenity's red curls, like Ross. She takes after her father.

Oliver and Loveday are fulfilling the prophecy he made before their wedding. "Offspring aren't all that love begets," he assured Loveday. "Hope, understanding, sympathy—we're not too old to beget these."

Oliver is too old to work much outdoors now. He spends his days in his study at Firbank Farm, writing to Quaker farmers all over the country. "Lethal agents employed in warfare are rendering parts of the world incapable of sustaining life, even after hostilities have ceased," he tells them. "Some researchers are hoping to reverse the damage. Would you lend them a patch of land for a year or so to test their theories?"

Faster than Oliver is able to write, farmers are responding with offers of acreage and, though he didn't ask for it, money. Young Friends everywhere are organizing work camps to carry out the experiments.

Loveday has her hands full, too. She's coordinating the project.

The Friends Hostel, which Serenity and Peter Holland were running as a shelter for homeless people, had to close. Those who drifted in needed more support than Friends were capable of giving—psychiatric counseling and long-term security. The Hollands had put their hearts into the effort. When it proved untenable, they felt defeated.

Then, just after little Daphne was born, Professor Anselm, the forester who was the first to recognize the value of Oliver's formula for restoring defoliated vegetation in Vietnam, approached Kendal Meeting. Might the hostel be used for a new study? If successful, it would make soil, which has been rendered unfit to produce food, fertile again.

After giving the matter prayerful consideration, Kendal Friends approved. Peter is directing the project. Serenity and others are assisting him. Results of the first experiments are very promising.

That's what's happening in Kendal at present.

I'd like to be there, listening to what Ross has to say after his first day at school. I wish I could take little Daphne's hand as she starts walking. And I'd give anything to be at Firbank with Oliver and Loveday, watching them live each hour in an aura of happiness.

But no. At least not now.

For it has just come to me that this is the moment to glance back, not to recount the events of my life, as one does in an autobiography, but simply to trace the influences that, I believe, made me into a writer. I spoke of these influences in Greensboro and Providence, Rhode Island, when I addressed the Conference of Quaker Historians and Archivists.

While I was giving those talks, it suddenly struck me that I had never spoken so freely to my family as I was speaking to total strangers.

I had always assumed that my children and grandchildren would be bored if I were to run on about my work. But would they? Maybe growing up in my eighties means being less reticent with those I love.

I made a resolution. I'd write an account of my literary life, not for publication, just for my family. It would be more extensive than the talks and far more personal.

At once, the opening words of John Woolman's *Journal* came into my mind:

I have often felt a motion of love to leave some hints in writing of my experience of the goodness of God and now, in the thirty-sixth year of my age, I begin this work.

More than twice as old as Woolman was then, I had never kept a journal and didn't plan to. Yet, I felt a deep "motion of love" to convey the "experience of the goodness of God" that writing has been for me.

Speaking about myself has never been easy. When people ask how I got my start or how I devise plots and create characters, I'm struck dumb. I can't explain that I still feel like a beginner, that the characters come to life and act of their own accord, without interference from me.

Still, I'd made that resolution. So how did I begin? Who inspired me?

Of the many people who illuminated my path along the way, a few unconsciously struck the spark that enkindled particular books. While their likenesses never appear, some element of their personalities touches the pages. Who were these people? Which books did they influence?

Without having known the English children who came to New Haven during the Blitz, I couldn't have written *Now That April's There*. Without the friendship of Westerly Friends, I wouldn't have been inspired to write the Kendal novels. Without having lived with 102 undergraduate women for five years, when I myself was in my fifties, I couldn't have written *Mount Joy* or *I Take Thee, Serenity* or *The Wondrous Gift*.

And without the love George bestowed upon me when we were in our seventies, I never would have written *Indian Summer of the Heart*. George gave me the end of a golden string. It led me in at Heaven's gate.

There were many others who animated my vision. When I fumbled and the little ball went scuttling off into a dark corner, they got down on hands and knees and retrieved it. I wish I could thank each one.

You are still upholding me, dear children and grand-children, friends, editors, responsive readers, even you who now live only in memory.

This is my love letter to all of you.

These are the books
(not counting *Things That Never Happened*)—

Timothy Travels
Sperli the Clockmaker
Now That April's There
Diligence in Love
The Autumn's Brightness
Mount Joy
A Procession of Friends
I Take Thee, Serenity
Indian Summer of the Heart
The Wondrous Gift (novella)
A Golden String

1

Maybe the teachers in the ten schools I went to didn't really think I was hopeless, but that's what many of them communicated to me. And I must have been a trial. Often, I didn't know what I was supposed to have learned in their school the year before because I hadn't been there. I was the new girl, behind in the work, sometimes a foreigner.

My parents travelled a great deal on account of my father's textile importing business. I suspect it was the other way around—that he chose his occupation because it obliged him to do what he loved to do: travel.

The whole first year of their married life, my parents spent going around the world. They were Americans, but they settled in France, where my brother Walter was born. Five years later, they moved to the north of England, where I was born in Southport, Lancashire, on the coast of the Irish Sea.

Having lived in France so long, my parents tended to speak French at home, even in England. It seemed quite logical to them that French should be the language I must learn first. So there I was, a little American, babbling French, while, all around us, people spoke English with a Lancashire accent, like the Beatles.

My father and mother spoke German, too, usually when they didn't want me to understand what they were saying. No greater incentive for my trying to learn a language could have been devised. I can't remember a time when I wasn't trilingual, though I never learned grammar, not even the English.

All this may have had something to do with my becoming a writer. At an early age, I discovered that I couldn't just blurt out the first words that came into my head. I had to remember to choose an appropriate vocabulary, depending on the place I was in and the person I was addressing.

This last—the need to consider the other person—seems particularly relevant to novel writing. From my earliest years, I had to imagine myself in the thinking and feeling of others. Almost more than the ability to communicate with words, this awareness of another's situation, the unconscious projection of oneself into the personality of someone else, is a faculty essential to the novelist.

I was too young when we left Southport to remember the town. But, the year I was fifty-one, when I was visiting friends in the north of England, I went there out of curiosity. The bus stopped in front of the library. On impulse, I went in.

An exhibit of books by local authors was ranged in the vestibule. I couldn't believe my eyes: there were the British editions of the first two Kendal novels—*Diligence in Love* and *Dilly,* as *The Autumn's Brightness* was called in England! I was considered a local author!

What would my parents have said, had they foreseen this in 1904? My mother's only prediction on beholding me is reported to have been, "The pillar of my old age."

Walking on the Promenade in Southport, where I had been wheeled as an infant, I wondered whether it was this early influence that gave me and my seafaring descendants a lifelong love of the sea.

My father commuted to Manchester. Fog was an ever-present hazard, enveloping the mill towns inland. A man would walk ahead of the train with a lantern. It took all morning to travel the fifty miles. My father just had time to go to his office, collect the mail, and start home again.

When we moved to London, we lived in Linden Gardens,

Bayswater. I spent my days in Kensington Gardens with Peter Pan, who was also born in 1904. That gave us a special bond. He must have influenced me, for I never lost the desire to preserve the wonder and simplicity of a child's world.

By the time I went to Kensington Gardens, I was quite big enough to walk, but my nanny delayed my maturing by pushing me in the pram so she wouldn't have to clean my white shoes.

When I was three and a half, my mother took me to New York to meet my grandmother and my aunts and uncles. We sailed from Liverpool on the maiden voyage of the first *Mauretania*, returning on the *Lusitania*. My impression of America was delightful: I had my first taste of ice cream.

Apart from that short visit, I was never in the United States until I started school in Yonkers, outside of New York. Incredible as it may seem, that was almost country then. The people in Yonkers thought my British accent very amusing. I got rid of it as fast as I could.

My brother Walter was ridiculed even more because his clothes had been bought in London and they weren't like those the boys on our block were wearing.

But that didn't last long. The next year, my parents took me back to Europe. Walter was left behind with an uncle and aunt. His education was important and mustn't be interrupted. Mine never mattered.

My father went to Europe on business twice a year. My mother and I would sail over with him and wait for months in Switzerland or France, while he travelled around Europe and then went back to the States to take care of things there. It was a hard separation, not mitigated as it would have been today by telephone contact or airmail.

Each time we went abroad, we gave up our house and stored the furniture. I still remember the anguish of moving day, of watching my bed and the tuck box, in which I kept my toys, being carted off by strange men. Home was no longer where it was supposed to be. When we returned, we moved into a new place, never in the same familiar neighborhood.

The year I was seven, when my mother and I were spending the winter above Montreux, waiting for my father to return from the States, my mother became so ill that she had to enter a sanatorium. Institutions like that one, which undertook to cure patients of whatever their ailment might be through massage and mineral baths, flourished at that time.

I was allowed to share my mother's room. Where else could I have gone? We didn't know a soul in Switzerland. Besides, my mother needed me. I felt a great responsibility.

From our room, we looked out on the Lake of Geneva and the Dents du Midi, the chain of snow-capped mountains above the French shore. In the clear Alpine light, the view was indescribably beautiful. The mountains were like huge, friendly dogs, lying protectively around us.

But the view was frightening, too, for the Castle of Chillon lay directly below, on a little point that jutted out into the lake.

I had been taken to see the dark dungeon where Bonivard was imprisoned during the wars of the Reformation. Marks in the stone floor, supposedly his footprints, made as he paced his narrow cell four centuries earlier, were pointed out to tourists, especially the English, who piously quoted Byron:

> Chillon! thy prison is a holy place
> And thy sad floor an altar, for 'twas trod
> Until his very steps have left a trace
> Worn as if thy cold pavement were a sod,

By Bonivard! May none those marks efface!
For they appeal from tyranny to God.

I couldn't bear to look down at the stark castle. This was my first intimation that people might actually inflict pain wilfully on others. It was too terrifying. Something like that might happen to me and those I loved. The protecting mountains never calmed this fear.

To get to school, I had to take the funicular railway up the mountainside. That was fun.

In the sanatorium, the only contact I had with another child was when I was invited to play with the resident physician's little girl, who was much younger. An American patient must have pitied my loneliness. He taught me to play solitaire.

The massage and mineral baths did the trick. Or perhaps it was the news that my father was coming. Anyhow, by the time he arrived and took us to Paris, my mother was feeling better.

2

In Paris, I rolled my hoop in the Tuileries or watched Guignol, while my mother sat on a bench and embroidered. After dinner, the three of us went to one of the cafes on the Boulevard. My father always dipped a lump of sugar into his little coffee cup for me.

It was in the Paris cafes that I learned very early about the demimondaines, not about their gainful occupation—I had no idea what it was—but that certain women were set apart from my mother and the ladies we associated with. My parents would spot one amongst the couples sitting at the little round tables and would communicate the intelligence to each other with their eyes, never dreaming that I'd intercept the message. While I didn't know what differentiated those women, I soon recognized them by their bizarre makeup.

Travel exposed me to many of the realities of life that I might not have encountered had my childhood been spent at home. Yet, in a curious way, I also remained surprisingly innocent. I inhabited a secret world.

When it came time for my father to leave us again, my mother and I stayed in Chatou, near Paris. Some Scottish women, who ran a finishing school for English girls and didn't have enough students, took us in.

This was a lot more cheerful. Instead of the sick people we had been living among in Switzerland, we were surrounded by exuberant young women, who weren't taking their higher education too seriously. They only needed a smattering of French and knowledge of a few culinary arts before they were free to return home, fully equipped for marriage.

There was an ancient *glycine* by the front door of the school. It must have been in full bloom when we arrived because wisteria still has happy associations for me. The clusters of delicate purple flowers, the sweet, permeating scent still carry me back to those days in Chatou. When I was grown up and had children and a garden of my own, I put in wisteria, just as I tried to grow English lavender and laburnum.

In Chatou we had friends, an English family my parents had known when they lived in Paris. These people sometimes invited my mother and me to tea. I played with Graham, who was about my age. That was superb.

On my eighth birthday, I was given another of the sailor dresses I wore in those days and some new high-button shoes. My father arrived and presented me with a red morocco manicure kit. He had decided, after inspecting my fingernails, that that was what I ought to be wishing for. I soon managed to lose the manicure kit, but the necklace of tiny silver pansies, which he also gave me that day, still lies in my jewelry box, never worn, but treasured these seventy-odd years.

While I was taken to endless art galleries in our travels, Renoir's pictures were not brought to my attention. My parents, like many of their generation, considered the Impressionists too far out.

But when I began to educate myself, Renoir held an unaccountable fascination for me. I realize now that it was because he captured the mood of the landscape and the types I was at home with in France, in those unclouded days before the First World War.

Renoir loved Chatou: the Seine and the oarsmen in their narrow, red rowing boats. They wore white jackets with black ties and straw boaters. Renoir painted the patches of light made by the eddies in the river, the swaying grasses on the bank, the mystery conveyed by the atmosphere.

The picture of those oarsmen hangs in the National Gallery in Washington. It shimmers with enchantment. So does my recollection of Chatou.

Like the French children, I went to school enveloped in a black overall with a satchel on my back.

We didn't have individual seats and desks in that school, the way they had in the States. Four or five children sat on a long form at a continuous desk. Our dejeuner consisted of a hard roll with a thin piece of chocolate stuck in the middle—unwholesome and delicious.

Speaking the language gave me no trouble. I had learned it by ear, though, and knew nothing about spelling and the rules of grammar. These struck me as irrelevant, anyway.

I did have a very serious difficulty in that school. If I had stayed there longer, it might have proved disastrous.

In those days, the French considered left-handedness an aberration. It was sinister, gauche, and a conscientious teacher did her best to break a child of the habit. I'm not ambidextrous, so my teacher didn't succeed. But I tried hard to imitate the little girls on either side of me.

I don't remember any of them. One of the boys, Lionel, made a big impression. He had blond curls and still needed his afternoon nap.

Miss Strang, one of the mistresses in the school where we were living, gave me lessons in English. She let me write with my left hand. When I was about to leave for America, she wrote a poem in my notebook. I thought it a masterpiece and still recall it:

> Daisy and I have had good fun
> And we some very good work have done.

> When she is across the sea,
> I hope she will sometimes think of me.

I do, lovingly.

Back in New York, nobody minded about left-handedness. But we had penmanship—the Palmer Method, a circular motion. We had to make ellipses between horizontal lines—pages and pages. If you were normal, you could do this as far as your arm would reach, but if you were left-handed, you soon got stuck, stopped by your own body.

The girls had sewing. When I was in trouble and brought my work up to the teacher, she would say, "Go back to your seat. I can't help you."

This soon passed. We went to Europe again. And that time my mother and I accompanied my father. We moved around so much that I wasn't sent to school! Travel, my parents declared, was the best education. From my point of view, it was certainly the most pleasant.

We went to Italy, to Belgium and Holland, where I was entranced by the wooden shoes and native costumes. We went sightseeing, to museums and concerts, to bookshops and theaters. Everywhere, I tried to learn the language by studying street signs and notices in shop windows or buses.

The museums affected me much as the Castle of Chillon did earlier. All those paintings of the Crucifixion, the Crown of Thorns, very bloody, the suffering of the saints. I hurried past Rembrandt and Rubens—portraits of burghers so dressed up that they looked stiff—to Franz Hals and Breughel, who celebrated the joy of life. These appealed to me.

The French plays were chosen for my parents' entertainment and were, they must have hoped, over my head. They were indeed, but I enjoyed the acting and took in the portrayal of personality.

Moving about that way, I rarely got to know other children. I was just with grown-ups. Looking out of train windows and from the decks of ocean liners, I dreamed. In the hotels and pensions we stayed in, I watched the other guests, listened to them, as they spoke their various languages, and tried to imagine who they were.

Perhaps these early experiences enabled me later to get inside the minds of my characters. But if the enforced observation was good training for a future writer, it did nothing to satisfy my teachers. Whichever country I was in, they found my ignorance exasperating.

Still, I must have learned more than they gave me credit for. In any case, when I listen today to the complaints of children and their parents, or read about the Boston School Committee, I'm not sure that my eclectic and peripatetic education was so bad.

The outbreak of the First World War brought a temporary halt to our wandering. I was ten years old. For the first time in my life, I stayed in my own country long enough to put down some roots.

3

When war broke out in Europe and we were grounded in New York, I began to participate in the life of my contemporaries. On Washington Heights, where we lived, there was so little traffic that we kids played in the street—hopscotch and prisoner's base, all new to me and very exciting. Opposite our house, there were four blocks of vacant lots where we could run around, except in the week during the summer when Billy Sunday pitched his tent there and held revival meetings.

I began to have friends, went roller skating, and, best of all, helped myself to any book I fancied on the shelves of the public library. Sunday mornings, the whole family walked in Fort Tryon Park, now the site of The Cloisters, or we went down to the little lighthouse on the Hudson.

For reasons I can't fathom—a shift in population, perhaps, or the whim of Tammany Hall—some of the instability of my schooling persisted. I was assigned to three different public schools before we moved further downtown, when I had to switch again. The curriculum was, of course, the same in all of them, but the buildings and the teachers were strange.

Even before the United States entered the war, my parents grieved over it. Places they knew and loved had been invaded. Their friends were losing sons. I used to be sent out to buy the evening paper at the newsstand on Broadway. Running home, I anticipated the terror with which my father would snatch the paper out of my hand to scan the ghastly headlines.

His business came to a standstill. Mills all over Europe, which had supplied the textiles he imported, were converted to munitions factories. Desperate, my father looked around for some other means of supporting us.

He began sending chemicals to Italy. He knew nothing about that business but he spoke Italian fluently and could locate the items Italian firms wished to buy in the United States. Then he discovered that some of the chemicals he was being asked to ship, while harmless themselves, were being combined with others for the manufacture of explosives.

Walter had enlisted. My father, unwilling to profit from the sale of materials that might be used to kill another man's son, refused to fill the orders. His business collapsed. For the remainder of the war, our financial situation was precarious.

Years later, when I came amongst Friends and grasped the awesome implications of the Quaker Peace Testimony, I realized that I had already been indoctrinated.

Finally, the nightmare was over. Walter was released from the service. My father slowly rebuilt his business. It was not yet sufficiently active to warrant his engaging a secretary when he became very ill.

I was a freshman at Hunter College High School. When I came home in the afternoon, I sat by my father's bedside while he dictated his business letters in four languages. When he had checked my shaky spelling, I transcribed the letters on his old portable, feeling very grown-up.

The teaching at Hunter didn't inspire me. Myra, my camp counsellor, who later became my sister-in-law, urged me to apply to the Ethical Culture School, from which she had graduated. This was one of the rare private schools that accepted students of whatever race, religion, social position, or ability to pay. The affluent parents contributed to the tuition of children who would otherwise not have been able to attend, so fees were unusually high. My parents could not have afforded that.

Summoning courage, I went to the school by myself and asked for a scholarship. I was granted a partial one. My parents could pay the rest.

In this, my tenth school, I was supremely happy. At the time, I knew nothing about Friends schools. Now, having been a trustee of three of them, I realize that I would have been equally happy in a Friends school. But when I entered Ethical, the idealism there seemed unique.

Begun in 1878 on the Lower West Side as the Workingman's School for the children of unemployed printers, it first made sure that the students were adequately nourished. Highly qualified teachers were found to teach not only academic subjects but manual skills. The well-to-do members of the Ethical Culture Society, who were supporting the school, soon realized that the children of the poor were getting a better education than their own children.

Recalling this in his *Story of the School,* Felix Adler, the founder, wrote that "it became evident that a class school, whether for the rich or the poor is a mistake. In a democracy, children of all classes must early be brought into contact with one another."

Renamed the Ethical Culture School, it moved to Sixty-third Street, overlooking Central Park. It had no playground. We played on the roof.

By the time I entered the school, Dr. Adler was a very old man, at least so he looked to me—wispy, with the pink skin and innocent expression of a baby. Reading his educational philosophy now, I'm struck by its resemblance to the Quaker principles I've tried to interpret in the Kendal novels.

"Every human child appeared as a kind of Christ child," he wrote. "A light seemed to stream from it, not indeed that of actual divinity but of divine possibilities often hidden. . . . The task of education thus seemed that of penetration, revelation turning potentialities into potencies."

I went to school on the subway in rush hour. There were so many people, the doors wouldn't close. Guards ran down the platform, shoving us in. I thought it was great!

I stayed at Ethical two years and had none of the trouble with the teachers I had had in previous schools, only with the janitor. When he locked up at night, there weren't supposed to be any kids left in the building and I didn't want to go home.

Senior year, Mr. Hutchins taught me English. He was the first teacher who ever gave me the sense that I had "potentialities" and who tried to turn them into "potencies."

He was working for his Ph.D. at Columbia. Once he invited me there for a lecture by Mark Van Doren. I recall my excitement at being in a university lecture hall. Me, just a high school kid!

At Ethical, we had weekly ethics classes. John Lovejoy Elliott, who lived and worked among the poor in Hell's Kitchen, challenged us to distinguish between right and wrong in hypothetical situations. Up to that time, I had been told what was right and what was wrong. Suddenly, I was encouraged to figure things out for myself. I found it exhilarating.

"Live in promoting the best life in others," Dr. Adler urged. "Make manifest your true self in evoking the highest self in your fellows."

This sounds like a humanist paraphrase of the words of George Fox: "Then you will come to walk cheerfully over the world, answering that of God in every one; whereby in them ye may be a blessing, and make the witness of God in them to bless you."

The ground was clearly being prepared for what I was later to hear Friends refer to as "the Seed."

In that school, I had come to a place where my idealism and sensitivity were not only accepted but affirmed.

Unfortunately, there were also required subjects for which I had no aptitude, notably math and physics. Geometry—that I was able to pass by doggedly memorizing. None of it went into my head. I just stared at the theorems until I was able to reproduce them and so I squeaked by. But physics! I had no idea what was going on.

Mr. Klock was not only an outstanding physics teacher, he was kind. He did what he could, but I was hopeless.

One of my classmates was J. Robert Oppenheimer. No wonder I wasn't able to keep up!

Not long ago, I was asked by Bob's biographer to contribute my recollections of the boy who was to become a great atomic scientist. Apart from the impression that he had been extremely friendly and modest about his superior intelligence, I had little to offer. What I remembered chiefly was the configuration of Bob's ears.

Being incapable of understanding most of what went on in physics class, I observed the people around me, the way I used to do in my travels. Looking up and down the lab, I compared my classmates' ears.

I transmitted the results of my physiognomical research to Bob's biographer. When the book came out, I was not surprised that this vital bit of information had been withheld.

Mr. Klock gave me the final exam three times. After the last attempt, when I seemed not to have done any better, he said—he must have been weary—"I don't think it's altogether charity to say you've passed."

The College Entrance Board was less compassionate.

Although Mr. Hutchins, my English teacher, encouraged me, I never, so far as I can recall, thought of writing for fun in those days. My head wasn't full of fantasies. Music was my passion. So was drawing.

Herbert, my artist friend, took me to the country and

taught me to sketch with pencils. He made the most beautiful scenes of old farms and tumble-down houses. I was more interested in people and longed to do portraits but was too self-conscious to ask anyone to pose for me.

My ambition was realized years later, when I began to write novels. Using words instead of pencils, I made portraits of people I saw with my inner vision, not actual people. So I didn't have to ask anyone to pose.

Music—that was my first love. I practiced the piano with gusto. I wasn't aware of my rather poor coordination or of the fact that, unlike others, I had less dexterity in the treble than in the bass. All I knew was that playing the piano made me happy. I loved my teacher, Katie. If someone with roughly the same proficiency as mine consented to play a Beethoven symphony four hands with me—that was bliss.

I was born too early to have grown up with good recordings and radio. We did have a phonograph but it didn't reproduce tone accurately. From the time I was thirteen, my mother and I had season tickets for the New York Philharmonic. Later, I went to recitals by myself.

Perhaps because good music wasn't so easy to come by, I developed the habit of listening intently. That may be the reason why I now find it impossible to concentrate on anything else when music is being played. It's not background for me. My children and grandchildren keep their radios going while they work. They say it helps them to think. It just drives me crazy. I'm forced to stop everything and listen, the way I did in my youth, when, after riding the streetcar to Fifty-seventh Street and walking over to Carnegie Hall against the wind blowing off the East River, I had the rapture of hearing Paderewski or Casals or Kreisler or young Heifetz.

Mr. Hutchins urged me to apply to college. He was an

enthusiastic Yale man. So that was my first choice. But it would be almost half a century before Yale admitted women. Long before that, my wish to be there was vicariously realized when I became a faculty wife.

With Mr. Hutchins's alma mater beyond my reach, I decided to apply to the next best school, in my estimation—Harvard.

Harvard College didn't admit women, either. But a few enlightened members of the faculty, who were perhaps in need of a small second salary, walked over to Radcliffe, which was at a discreet distance from the Harvard Yard. There they repeated for the benefit of the women the lectures they had already given to the men. This equal-but-separate instruction prevailed for twenty years after my time.

I applied to Radcliffe although my parents were reluctant. They didn't want me to go away to college. Why couldn't I get just as good an education at Barnard? Columbia University was within walking distance of our house. I could live at home.

To me, it seemed that living at home while I went to college would be like attending yet another elementary or secondary school—my eleventh. However, considering my grade in physics, which was just below passing, I didn't have much hope of being accepted at Radcliffe.

Of course, when I was asked on the application form why I wished to go there, I didn't admit that it was because I couldn't go to Yale. Young New Yorker that I had become, I answered, "Because it's in the country."

4

The first to put a golden string into my hand was a little girl of six named Eleanor. There may have been someone who inspired me earlier, but Eleanor was the first person who moved me to make a book. The whole limited edition—three volumes—is still extant. Eleanor has one. I have the other two. Bound over sixty years ago, they are in surprisingly good condition.

Radcliffe College accepted me. The College Board grade in English evidently made up for the one in physics. My parents agreed to my going, on the condition that I only stay a year. I, of course, secretly hoped that, at the end of that time, they would relent.

When I arrived in September, I was given a room on the ground floor of Barnard Hall, overlooking the hockey field. I used to stand at the window, watching the Cambridge kids cutting across the grass on their way to the public school.

One little girl especially attracted my notice. She was very pretty, with long yellow braids and high coloring. Like me, she was left-handed. I knew this because one morning she was throwing stones at the boys. Shocked, I ran out and discovered that her right sleeve was sewed up just below the elbow. She had lost the hand. The boys seemed to think this misfortune entitled them to make fun of her. So she threw stones at them.

This, at least, is my recollection. Eleanor insists that she never did anything like that. And she must know.

Later, I invited her into my room. She wasn't just pretty. There was a merry expression in her blue eyes, a desire to communicate, to share a joke, which overcame her shyness. I began writing stories for her.

One afternoon, when Eleanor was going home from school, I ran out and gave her a sheaf of pages held together with paper fasteners. These, as far as I can recall, were the first stories I ever wrote.

Cambridge was a quiet, unsophisticated town in those days. A little girl could play safely in front of her house on Garden Street, between Christ Church, where General Washington worshipped, and the huge elm, under whose branches he took command of the Continental army. The elm has long since been cut down. Only a bronze plaque, embedded in the road, remains to mark the spot. No one can read the plaque because cars are continually running over it. But in 1922, the elm still stood in all its glory just beyond the Radcliffe Yard.

Biking down Garden Street one afternoon (bareheaded, in defiance of college rules!) I saw Eleanor playing on the Common across from her house and stopped to speak to her. Eleanor's mother, watching over her from the parlor window, was anxious to know the stranger who befriended her child. She invited me in. Even Eleanor's doctor father came out of his office to meet me. Her brothers lurked in the hall, at the foot of the circular staircase, which was one of the features of the old Cambridge houses.

Eleanor wanted to impress me with how well she was reading. I can still see her, standing by the fireplace in that parlor with a sheaf of pages propped in the crook of her afflicted arm, proudly reading my stories, to the delight of her parents and brothers and my great embarrassment.

In the spring of the year, I met Dick. He was a freshman at Harvard, hoping to go to medical school and become a pediatrician. I liked his Southern courtesy and his whimsical notions. He felt attracted to the cosmopolitan world I lived in, so different from his Texas culture.

It was important to me that Dick, who loved children,

meet my little friend. So we took Eleanor to the old Cock Horse for lunch. I remember how sweet she was, what fun we had with her.

The few months that remained of the term were, except for weekends, the only time Dick and I spent in the same place until our marriage five years later.

At the end of my freshman year, Walter and Myra were married. My parents claimed that they were entitled to have one child at home. Although I had been warned, this was a blow. I was happy at Radcliffe and had made friends. I left, believing that I would never return.

I never did, as a student. But how surprised I would have been had I been able to look into the future! Eventually, I returned in three other capacities: as a parent, as head resident of Holmes Hall and director of the Radcliffe College Music Center, and, when I moved to Lincoln, as an affiliate of North House, which by then was part of Harvard.

Back in New York, the summer I was nineteen, I wanted a job. But I didn't know how to go about finding one. I turned to my old teacher, Mr. Hutchins.

He really must have believed in me for he gave me an introduction to Henry Seidel Canby, who was then editing the *Literary Review,* and told me to present his card at the editorial office.

The idea of doing something so daring scared me. "Oh no," I cried, "I couldn't do that. I couldn't possibly."

Mr. Hutchins laughed. "What are you afraid of?" he asked. "Do you think Mr. Canby will steal your carfare so you won't be able to get home?" Put that way, my fear sounded pretty silly.

Mr. Canby was kind, too. He had no job for a youngster without experience or a college degree, only a knowledge of a few languages, but he gave me a book to review, the first of several. This was a new translation of *The Adventures of Baron Munchausen*, which I had read in German. Another new translation he asked me to review was *Heliodorus: An Ethiopian Romance*. The first English translation had been made in 1587.

When this review appeared, there was my name, in print! Even more important, I was paid three dollars. That made me a professional writer, didn't it?

In the fall, I enrolled at Barnard College, singing in the choir of St. Paul's Chapel for part of my tuition. By midyear, this fizzled out, too. My parents wanted me to go abroad with them. I didn't mind leaving Barnard. I had more grandiose aspirations.

If I was going to be in Europe, why couldn't I study literature at Oxford? My little reviews had given me the idea that I might become a writer. Where but at Oxford would I get the best preparation? If I could just get in, if I could just persuade my parents—

They weakened. They agreed to my going, although my mother declared that she would not spend another winter in England. She had had quite enough of that climate when we lived there.

Somerville, Lady Margaret Hall, St. Hugh's, St. Hilda's— not one of the residential women's colleges at Oxford considered me. But the Society of Home Students—now St. Anne's College—agreed to let me take the entrance exams, which were given in April. If I passed, I would be eligible for Responsions, the University exams, given in September. The Home Students, I was informed, either lived at home or in digs.

Unlike the British students, who had been preparing for

Oxford since infancy, I had no idea what to expect from those exams. I was allowed to take them in Paris. Because we arrived late, I had to cram all of them into three days.

When I heard that I had passed, I could hardly believe it. My educational fortunes were about to change!

Mother and I went to Switzerland and settled down for the summer in a hotel in Engelberg, above the Lake of Lucerne, hoping that the mountain air and sunshine would improve her health.

All day long, I studied. Latin was my greatest worry. I hadn't had nearly so much preparation as the students from the British schools. Although I was lugging a heavy suitcase full of textbooks around Europe, I found I lacked what I needed most—a grammar. Where would I find that in a hamlet on the mountainside?

There was, I discovered, a Benedictine monastery within walking distance. Dare I go there and ask the Brothers to lend me a Latin grammar? The porter at the hotel warned me that those Benedictines were very strict. They might not open the door to a young girl.

I tugged at the doorbell several times. Nothing happened. Someone was peeping through a grating. Finally, the door was opened. The peeper hid. Behind an iron gate at the top of a long staircase stood an unsmiling monk. In German I asked if I might borrow a Latin grammar.

The monk said, "Come back tomorrow."

I went back. The door was opened just wide enough for a book to be passed through. I took it gratefully and left as fast as I could.

When I was sick of studying, I walked, feeling guilty, and made pencil sketches of the mountains, the way my friend Herbert had taught me to do. How perverse life can be! All that Latin did nothing to help me become a writer, but those sketches I made when I was playing hooky in Engelberg would, only four years later, appear as illustrations in my first book.

The main thing that Switzerland did for us with respect to health that summer was to give me what I later learned was an iodine deficiency. The glands in my neck swelled.

In September, we spent some days in Paris. Mother took me to see the doctor who had taken care of her when she lived there, long before I was born.

He declared gravely that I was threatened with tuberculosis. I must rub my chest with alcohol twice a day. Staunch Frenchman that he was, he described in grim detail what would happen if I subjected my health to the rigors of the English climate. Under no circumstances was I to go to Oxford.

5

Naturally, I ignored the doctor. Well, not quite. I was pretty scared. Still, not go to Oxford, after persuading my parents? After passing those first exams?

I expected my mother to be so upset that she'd insist on my staying in Paris with her. But I was wrong. She knew how much going meant to me. And I don't think she quite believed the doctor. His diagnostic method—guesswork—was clearly out of date.

It was very loving of my mother not to rationalize. Her brother had died of tuberculosis during his medical internship. She might easily have told herself that keeping me with her would be best for me. All she said was, "See how you feel. If you have any trouble, don't stay. And get some rubbing alcohol as soon as you arrive. Use it regularly."

The Channel was rough. I just managed not to be seasick.

In the train at Paddington, there was a friendly clergyman from Yorkshire. He had been an undergraduate at Oxford and he gave me an introduction to one of his professors. Dr. Simpson and his wife were, he said, interested in foreign students. They would enjoy my going to call.

Finding digs in Oxford wasn't easy. There was anti-American feeling left over from the war. "You came when all was over," a taxi driver, to whom I must have given too small a tip, taunted me. Landladies claimed Americans wanted too much light and too much heat. Besides, the girls weren't serious students. They only came to ensnare the dons.

I had no such intentions. But I did crave light enough to

study by and a little warmth. At last, I found a woman who had lived in Canada and was therefore sufficiently broad-minded to fill her house on Keble Road with American girls. Not one of us ensnared a don, at least not while I was there.

The best feature in that house certainly wasn't the food. It was the piano. I was allowed to play it in the evening.

Oxford was chilly. Wearing the warmest dress I had—a wine-red wool—I went to the Examination Schools in the High to take Responsions. No one had told me that the candidates were required to appear uniformly dressed. The boys all wore gray suits with white bow ties, the girls black or dark blue frocks. The British candidates knew this, of course. I was the only one in the huge hall who didn't conform.

Mortified, I tackled the Latin paper. It was worse than I'd feared. I was trying to remember the syntax in the grammar book I'd borrowed from the monks in Engelberg, when the proctor, impressive in his academic gown, strode up and unnerved me by demanding bitingly, "Aren't you rather gaily dressed for this occasion?"

The following day, when I took the literature exam, it was just as cold but I wasn't going to be mortified again.

One of the essay questions tested my integrity: Can England rightly be called a Christian nation?

What answer did the examiners want? Were they trying to ascertain my religious convictions? I was still trying to figure them out myself. I twiddled my fountain pen. If I said yes, would that get me a better grade? But I didn't really approve of a national religion.

Those ethics classes in high school had conditioned me. I had to tell the truth as I saw it. Bravely I answered, "No, not as long as there is poverty in England and she engages in war."

I thought, If the Latin hasn't already done me in, this will.

But I underestimated the examiners. Oxford University accepted me! I would have to be tutored in Latin, but I was on the road to securing a degree. For the next three years, the beauty that overwhelmed me every time I walked down the street would be mine to savor.

At the chemist shop in the Banbury Road, no one had ever heard of alcohol. I went to Boots in the Cornmarket. "Alcohol?" The clerk shook his head. No alcohol in Oxford? Impossible! It took a lot of searching before I discovered that I should have been asking for methylated spirits.

I rubbed my chest faithfully twice a day. The glands didn't respond.

The room on Keble Road wasn't very warm. There was a gas ring you turned on with a shilling, but it smelled so, I quickly turned it off.

Never mind, I didn't stay in the room much. Outdoors was so exciting! I rode my rented bicycle all over town, till I felt as at home in those streets as I did in New York. I biked along the Cherwell, or out past the colleges to Magdalen Bridge and on along the Isis.

Professor and Mrs. Simpson did indeed turn out to be hospitable. Middle-aged, with no children, they invited colonial students—Africans and Indians, even an American girl—to lunch.

When I saw a poster announcing that the Oxford Bach Choir was holding auditions for the Brahms Requiem, I screwed up my courage and tried out. I knew the music by heart, having sung it with the Radcliffe Choral Society, the Harvard Glee Club, and the Boston Symphony, under the direction of Serge Koussevitzky. Dick had come to each of the three performances.

The Oxford Bach Choir accepted me.

The various colleges had marvelous choirs. I went to

morning prayer and evensong, uplifted, not by the litany but by the boys' voices resounding in the vaulting.

I attended lectures on moral philosophy given in Hall at Pembroke, Dr. Johnson's college. What would he have said had he known that his college was being invaded by women? I attended lectures in German and heard one of the foremost Shakespeare scholars. Women, he said, were incapable of appreciating Shakespeare. They owed him so much and had done so little for his interpretation. To this was added the pronouncement that men were at their best amongst men, women in mixed company.

My expectations were so high! I wanted to be inspired, to have my imagination stirred. Maybe it was because I wasn't used to the British system, but the lectures left me cold. At that point, a tiny suspicion began timidly to assert itself: I might not have been cut out to be a scholar, after all. A writer's schooling might be elsewhere.

It was only a tiny suspicion, quickly put down by the beauty of the architecture and the historical aura that surrounded the colleges and their magnificent gardens. These really did stir and inspire me.

Then I came down with what we called "the grippe," together with a nasty cough. I stayed in my clammy bed, shivering. Long after I was up again, the cough persisted. It just wouldn't stop.

In the November rain and penetrating cold, I dragged myself to the lectures, staying outdoors no longer than I had to. Was that Paris doctor right? Could I really be getting TB? Was I endangering my health, as he predicted, by remaining in this climate?

My tutor was sympathetic. She tried to encourage me. At my age, she said a little wistfully, one gets over these things in no time.

But I didn't. I kept rubbing my chest till I thought the

skin would come off. The cough just got worse. It was embarrassing in the lectures.

I wrote to my mother. She was alarmed. Hadn't I better leave Oxford?

Leave? How could I?

My father had returned from the States. He wrote, too. Mother was going to the south of France. Sunshine would cure my cough. Hadn't I better go with her?

Never had I been so wretched. I couldn't blame my failure to stay in college on my parents this time. It was my own fault—the fear that, all my life, I might regret having obstinately pushed my luck too far.

I went to say good-by to the Simpsons. They had been very good to me.

Why, when life looks bleak, can't we see into the brightness of the future? I thought I was saying good-by forever.

How comforting it would have been at that moment to know that I'd continue calling on the Simpsons as long as they lived. And that, twenty-six years later, I would stay with them on my first trip to England after the Second World War; that Dr. Simpson would insist on bringing me breakfast in bed so I wouldn't know that I was being given their only rationed egg. And that Dick would telephone transatlantic in the middle of the night, scaring them out of their wits. He just couldn't wait till their daybreak to tell me that Doubleday was going to publish *Diligence in Love!*

It would have helped, too, if I could have known that my short stay in Oxford would enable me, when going there was out of the question because of the war, to picture Oxford, the setting for my first novel, and that that book would become a best-seller.

But I couldn't have that comfort then.

6

I joined my parents in Paris and took my mother to Nice. We spent the remainder of the winter in a hotel facing the Promenade des Anglais. Our window looked out on the Mediterranean. It was very beautiful. And yet, I was unhappy.

In the public rooms, I observed people. There was no one my age, no one I cared to talk to. Once again, I was that child who travelled with her mother, only now I was grown up. And whereas I'd been reasonably content before, now I felt that life had somehow cheated me.

What I missed most was a piano.

I went out and sketched, the way I'd done in Engelberg—the flower market in Nice, the roofs of Villefranche. These—if only I could have known it then!—would also illustrate my first book.

The cough did get better. The glands disappeared. But I had nothing to look forward to.

To distract myself, I began writing more of those fanciful children's stories and poems, all in the style of the little books my father used to read to me in my Edwardian nursery days: *The Sandwich Man, Balloons and Beanshooters, Churchmouse.*

Were they any good? Or hopelessly immature? How could I tell?

In the spring we went to Gurnigel in Switzerland. The morning after we arrived, when I opened the door of our hotel room, I heard the sound of a piano. Someone down the corridor was playing Beethoven—one of the sonatas. I stood still, enraptured. This was no young girl doing her morning practicing. It must be a concert artist.

At dinner, I noticed a distinguished-looking older man sitting at a table alone. The headwaiter told me he was Romain Rolland. An author! A real, live, famous author! I tried not to stare, but I wanted to meet him. I had read *Jean-Christophe* and some of his other books, including the little biography of Beethoven. Then I realized that it must have been M. Rolland who was playing that sonata. The head-waiter pointed me out to him. M. Rolland sent me a message, inviting me to tea in the lounge!

Romain Rolland was a charming person, tall, a little stooped, with arresting blue eyes, which spoke of suffering. I knew that he had had to leave France because of his pacifist stand during the war. He told me he lived in Villeneuve now, beyond the Castle of Chillon, at the end of the Lake of Geneva. His sister Madeleine lived next door. She would be coming next week and I must meet her. She had studied at Oxford and spoke English. He didn't.

I told him that I had written reviews, that I was hoping to be a writer. Very delicately, he let me know that I was not to go home and publish an article about him. I promised I wouldn't and I never did.

He told me about the book he was writing—an enlarged version of his biography of Beethoven. I couldn't wait to read it. (I still have that book, beautifully bound in leather, with love and Christmas greetings inscribed on the flyleaf by Leonora Lichnowsky, a descendant of Beethoven's patron, whom I had met somewhere in my travels.)

When M. Rolland's sister arrived, he invited me to join them on their walks. This was very different from the way I had felt in Nice. I was being accepted as a grown-up by people whom I regarded as models.

I can't quite explain what the meeting with my first author did for my artistic development. It was the quality of his personality that affected me, his integrity and musicianship and his willingness to suffer for advocating brotherhood among nations. This impression is still with me. His emphasis on characterization in his novels, now considered old-fashioned, may even have colored my style, when I began to write.

But, when I met him, I saw no future for myself, either in writing or anything else.

Back in New York, I didn't know what I was going to do. With my inability to stay in college long enough to get a degree, few interesting occupations were open to me.

Still, a writer didn't need a B.A. Could I teach myself? Maybe. But how could I prove myself? One isn't a writer until one has published. And I hadn't written anything worthy of publication.

Henry Seidel Canby, Christopher Morley, Amy Loveman, and perhaps others had founded the *Saturday Review of Literature*. They continued to send me books to review. This pleased but also troubled me. I was criticizing other people's work when I hadn't learned to write myself. That didn't seem fair. Were critics unsuccessful writers?

I started to type the stories and poems I'd written in Nice, thinking I'd send Eleanor another sheaf of pages like the ones she read to me, standing by the fireplace in Cambridge.

Then I thought, why not illustrate the stories in watercolor and make them into a regular little book?

I knew nothing about bookbinding but I had collected handmade paper—Italian for the pages, French that would be just right for the cover. When the pages were nicely written on and illustrated, I sewed them together and pasted them between boards covered with beautiful marbled paper—swirls of plum and cobalt blue, with a touch of scarlet, eddies of russet subsiding to saffron.

The first line of one of the poems, carefully lettered in sepia ink, supplied a title: *Things That Never Happened.*

> Things that never happen
> Are the nicest things of all
> For since they haven't happened yet
> Perhaps sometime they may . . .

When the little book was finished, it struck me as so surprisingly nice that before sending it to Eleanor, I made a copy for myself. Then I wondered, was this worthy of conveying my gratitude to Mr. Hutchins? Should I make a third one for him? Would a Ph.D. care for a children's book? Well, if he didn't, he could throw it away.

Thirty years later, I discovered that Mr. Hutchins did indeed value that little book. Shortly before he died—by then I had published several volumes without having to manufacture them myself—he sent me the copy of *Things That Never Happened* I had made for him, saying it ought to be in my possession.

Eleanor cherished hers, too. Eight years ago, when I visited her and her husband in Connecticut, she took the little book down from the shelf and began reading her favorite poem to me:

> The folk who live in Italy
> Eat macaroni constantly.
> We cut it neatly with our knife
> And eat it just like beans and pork
> Or cauliflower or cheese or pie,
> In little pieces with our bread.
> But there the little boys and girls
> Wind it round and round their fork

Then hold it high
And tip their head
To catch the string as it uncurls.

Eleanor was sixty-one then, about to retire after years of service to the handicapped, yet what I saw when she read to me that day was the merry little girl standing by the fireplace in the parlor on Garden Street.

While I was making the book, the year I was twenty-one, I heard of a summer job. The Nantucket Yacht Club needed a girl to work at the soda fountain. It was expressly stated that she was not to mingle with the members and their guests. All she was supposed to do was dish up ice cream and mix sodas.

The pay was low and no living accommodation was provided. I'd never been to Nantucket. I wanted that job. The yachtsmen didn't interest me.

My father wouldn't let me apply, not because the job was menial—he wasn't like that. He simply felt that a young girl oughtn't to live in a rooming house and eat around.

Being a well-brought-up young lady in the Twenties surely was rough!

What a contribution to American literature was possibly lost that summer—the amusing sketches I might have written after work in my shabby rooming house, the observations of a young soda jerk with downcast eyes and open ears, who waited on the clubby Nantucket yachtsmen!

Later, I visited the Island under conditions my father would have approved. But the literary inspiration I went there for eluded me.

Then, more than fifty years later, when I was living in George's pre-Revolutionary saltbox and lovingly protected, inspiration came with such force that I was torn between writing and walking over the moors with my husband.

"Surprised by joy," I began *Indian Summer of the Heart* on my portable typewriter in the little upstairs bedroom with the sloping floor, the room that overlooks the garden.

But the summer I was twenty-one, when Nantucket was denied me, I had to do something to get on with my life. So I went to Harvard summer school. Living in Gore Hall, later one of the River Houses, and eating at Commons was respectable, at least in my father's eyes. I took two English courses, one given by a popular Harvard professor.

What made the summer memorable for me was not this celebrated teacher, but his unassuming section man, Mr. Hood, who later became dean of Trinity College. In my freshman year at Radcliffe, I had taken a course in poetics with him that left a mark on my subsequent writing. Mr. Hood taught me to listen to the sound of words—words by themselves and in combination—making me sensitive to the sonority of language, as I had previously only been to music. His immortality, like that of all great teachers, is assured. I never put two words on paper without listening to them with my inner ear and wondering whether they would be acceptable to Mr. Hood.

During summer school, I dropped in to see him in his office at Warren House. The floor was so strewn with books that one had to step carefully from one little bare spot to another. Mr. Hood communicated something besides sonority that summer—the art of storytelling. He leaned back in his swivel chair with his feet on the desk and told me about the movie he'd seen the previous evening in a way that was surely more gripping than the actual screen production.

At the end of the summer, I went home to all the same problems.

But something had happened. Mr. Hood had given me a letter of introduction to Maxwell Perkins, the famous editor at Scribner's. In the letter, my childish stories were praised with endearing yet quite unwarranted hyperbole.

For nearly sixty years, this letter has reposed in my file, unsealed, the stamp (two cents!) uncancelled. Why didn't I drop the letter in the mail chute beside the elevator in our apartment house? Was I too timid? Or did I realize that I couldn't live up to the exaggerated praise? Did I try to deliver it to Mr. Perkins, only to be refused admittance because he was not interested in youngsters who hadn't yet made a name?

That letter, while never dispatched, accomplished what Mr. Hood had hoped for. It got me an editor, simply by giving me confidence. It made me believe that I might have something of worth to offer, after all.

So one day I got on the subway with my little homemade book and took it to a publishing house. In the months that followed, I took it to lots of publishing houses. I never saw an editor. A secretary would come out to the reception room and take my treasure, saying, "Come back in three weeks."

Waiting was agony. Naturally, my parents were puzzled. What did I think I was going to accomplish? As they watched me struggle, they must have thought me a changeling, left in their flat in Southport in place of the sensible child theirs ought to have been.

They didn't discourage me. They liked having me around. Making a children's book must have seemed a harmless occupation, like hemstitching handkerchiefs, on which I spent my eyesight in those years—the proper pastime for a young lady of my generation who had a father or a husband to support her. She wasn't supposed to prepare for a career.

It would only, as my mother commented, when one of my friends went to work, "take the bread out of the mouth of some poor woman who needs a job."

At the end of those three hard weeks, I went back to the publishing house. The secretary came out from the editor's office and handed me my book the way she might have thrown a sheet of botched typing into the wastebasket.

I took the book somewhere else. The same thing happened.

Then, one day, at Macmillan, I was told that the editor wanted to see me! I was ushered into the office of Louise Seaman, probably the leading juvenile editor at that time and surely the kindest.

Her first words were the most wonderful I'd ever heard: "Sit down."

I was sitting in an editor's office!

Holding *Things That Never Happened* with the respect I thought it deserved, Miss Seaman said, "I can't use this. But I'm interested in someone who would make it. Why don't you write a book?"

A book! A real book! Miss Seaman believed I could write one.

That's how it all began—with a spirited little girl whose cheerful heart moved me to create a gift of love and an editor who was willing to give a youngster some attention.

7

All of a sudden, there I was, with limitless opportunity! I had only to produce that book. But how did one begin?

Instinctively I perceived—what I occasionally over-looked later, to my sorrow—that I must only choose a subject I really knew something about. Surely that was travel in Europe from a child's perspective. So soon after the First World War, not many American children had been abroad.

I took an afternoon tutoring job to earn my pocket money and demonstrate that I wasn't just spending my days fooling around with my father's old typewriter. That left the mornings free and I went to work.

This may well be my most autobiographical book, at least on the surface. A child travels around Europe with his mother. The child had to be a boy—girls, it was generally assumed, would like reading about him but boys wouldn't want to read about a girl. The routes my mother and I took are described in the book, which is illustrated with carefully drawn maps and some of the sketches I made in our travels.

But this child—Timothy Todd, I called him—isn't like me. He won't grow up to be an artist. He isn't visited by drives and dreams that none of the adults around him understand. He's an outgoing little fellow with plenty of curiosity and he makes friends with everyone he meets. In Nice, he has the good fortune to find a little American girl his age. She has an older brother, who takes Timothy camping with them, thus getting him away from parental supervision for a bit. The three meet up with gypsies and learn something of their language. (I had read George Borrow's *Lavengro* at Harvard summer school.)

The grown-ups in the book are pedantic. They regard travel as purely educational. The young people are fun. It's easy to see which age group I identified with.

Until now, I've never had the courage to open that book. It's not just this particular one that I dread confronting and judging with experienced eyes. I feel the same way about all my books. I don't dare reread them because I'll want to rewrite them, change things, carry the narrative forward into the present. Long after they've been fixed in print, my characters continue to live with me. They have further adventures that I'd like to record. But it's too late.

Now that I've faced this first book—*Timothy Travels,* I called it, adding a subtitle: *From the Mediterranean to the North Sea*—I find that it isn't so bad. A little on the dull side, maybe, but nothing to be ashamed of.

"Illustrations by the author," the title page reads. They're not masterpieces, those illustrations, yet they are worthy of the text. The book is dedicated to my parents.

The ending shows that already then I was deeply concerned about peace and international understanding. On their last night in Europe before sailing home (it would take them two weeks!), Mrs. Todd says to Timothy:

> The moon is shining down on us in Holland now; in a fortnight it will be shining down on us in America. If only the people of the earth could remember that the moon sheds equal radiance on all of them, they would never be jealous of each other and go to war.

And Timothy declares:

> I'm never going to fight any European. They've been too nice to me. I might have, before I came to Europe, because I didn't know them. But they were all so friendly . . . I wouldn't fight with any of

those people now. Some day I'm going around the world, and when I get to know all the other races, and find them as nice as the Europeans, I'll never fight anyone—never.

Dear Timothy Todd, my first hero! You're an old man now, pushing seventy. Have you kept your youthful idealism in a world riddled with violence?

When I wrote the book, I was twenty-one or -two, with no more training or experience than I had when I was writing those little stories. But now I had what every author needs at any stage in his or her career: constructive professional criticism. Miss Seaman sent the manuscript out to readers and let me see their comments, which I took to heart.

After much rewriting—I would be doing that all my life—I finally submitted an acceptable draft. It ran to 307 pages.

Macmillan agreed to publish it, but not for another year. Their current juvenile list, Miss Seaman explained, was complete. Was I content to wait? Or would I prefer to take the manuscript to a firm by the name of Coward-McCann, which was just starting? It was looking for children's books to make up the first list.

Of course I couldn't wait! *Timothy Travels* appeared in Coward-McCann's first catalogue, along with Wanda Gàg's *Millions of Cats.*

Only one review—a glowing one—is extant, saved by my dear mother in a big scrapbook she bought when I started to appear in print. She had my name embossed on the cover. At the time, I considered this vanity. Now that I'm looking back over my literary experience, I'm grateful for the record of events long forgotten.

Insignificant though it was, this first book earned a distinction none of my others ever achieved: in November

1928, when *Timothy Travels* appeared, I was invited to speak on CBS.

Back at Macmillan, Miss Seaman wasn't letting go of me entirely. I had told her that I was engaged to a medical student, that we planned to be married in March, that we were going to Freiburg in the Black Forest so Dick could study pathology.

The Black Forest! Miss Seaman was fascinated. That was where the cuckoo clocks came from, wasn't it? Why didn't I write a book about them while we were there? Nothing of the kind had been written for children. Unfortunately, Miss Seaman admitted, warning me that publication might prove difficult, there was still a great deal of anti-German sentiment. Perhaps by the time the book was written, it would have disappeared.

I could only think of the possibilities of such a story. It would be joyful, ringing with music, alive with folklore and the beauty of the countryside.

Even before it was written, Miss Seaman felt proprietary about this book. She wanted Macmillan to publish it. The contract with Coward-McCann for *Timothy Travels* must, she declared, stipulate that Macmillan would have the first refusal on my next book.

I knew nothing about publishing but I had heard lurid stories about the advantage that publishers took of ingenuous authors. Macmillan wouldn't have done anything like that to me, I was sure. But another publisher, one I didn't know . . . When I went to the Coward-McCann office, I wanted to take my father with me. He knew nothing about publishing, but he was grown up.

Wasn't I? Supposed to be, anyway. I had to handle these negotiations myself.

The contract, signed and sealed, was delivered the day before the wedding. I had become an author!

8

It was spring. We were in love and living in a picturebook town.

Freiburg was dominated by the Minster. All around were medieval houses with gabled roofs. The marketplace beside the Cathedral was crammed with farm folk, livestock, and masses of flowers. The slow simplicity of life in Freiburg pleased us.

We told ourselves that we weren't tourists. Dick was studying at the university. I roamed the countryside and travelled around the Black Forest on little toy trains, taking in local color, talking to people, learning as much as I could about cuckoo clocks.

The handcrafted clocks were no longer being made. I tried to find people who remembered having seen them produced in their childhood.

Way out in the forest, there was an old lady whose husband had collected clocks till he had what amounted to a museum. I went to her house and she showed me her treasures, winding them up so I could hear them play. The ingenious mechanisms were wholly beyond my comprehension but their music set me to imagining songs of the forest and the heart. I began writing under the spell of all this beauty.

Sperli the Clockmaker came down from the mountain with a bulging pack strapped to his back. It was full of cuckoo clocks. He brought them to Freiburg to sell to a merchant who kept a shop near the Minster Square.

That is how the book opens. The merchant hangs the clocks on the wall and winds one up.

When the minute hand reached the hour, a little tune began to play. A cuckoo had flown into the shop. Another bird answered his call. Then leaves rustled, a woodman whistled, and the fall of his ax echoed in the distance.

The children of Freiburg loved the Clockmaker. They called him Sperli, meaning "the sparrow," because he was perky and small. He was also full of fun.

"Sperli" became my pet name for Dick. The book is dedicated to "The Sparrow."

With the Clockmaker, I created the first of my lovable male characters. He is cheerful, whimsical, warmhearted, full of zest, and so devoted to his bit of landscape that he almost seems to have sprung out of it. As soon as he has sold his clocks, he goes looking for the children.

Most of the men in my later books are older—Warden Godstow in *Now That April's There,* Maris's grandfather in *Mount Joy,* Philip Ludlow and Oliver Otis in the Kendal novels, and Content's grandfather in *The Wondrous Gift.* Not so childlike as Sperli, they are equally lovable, full of gentle humor, with the spiritual depth I have found in many Friends.

To us, at twenty-three, Freiburg appeared to be an idyllic place. The scars of war and defeat, we told ourselves, were healing. We were too innocent to perceive that, on the contrary, there was a serpent lurking in this paradise that would destroy its integrity as well as millions of innocent people.

During an earlier stay in Freiburg, Dick had made friends with Gerhard, a delightful fellow student, whose home was there. When Dick returned two years later with me, Gerhard and his mother were most hospitable. We were very fond of them. They seemed to be broader in outlook and more international than anyone else we met in Germany.

At the end of the summer, we sailed home and set up housekeeping in Baltimore. Dick went back to Johns Hopkins and I worked on the book.

Music couldn't be reproduced by printing in those days. So I drew the notation for the tunes I wished to include, making the notes square, as I found them in ancient manuscripts.

As Miss Seaman had foreseen, publication took a long time. *Sperli the Clockmaker* didn't appear until the spring of 1932. It was beautifully illustrated in a woodcut style by Edward Thorne Thompson.

The review in the *New York Times,* also saved by my mother, praises the book. Indeed, in craftsmanship it is more mature than *Timothy Travels.*

A Freiburg publisher was interested in bringing out a German translation. We were in the process of negotiating when Hitler came to power and the correspondence ceased. But later the Junior Red Cross brought out an edition that pleased me more than any translation could have done. *Sperli the Clockmaker* was transcribed into Braille.

After the political upheaval in Germany, we lost sight of Gerhard. We weren't too concerned, as his family was not Jewish. It didn't occur to us that he might be in danger because of his liberal views. Then came the Second World War. We never heard from Gerhard again.

But well over forty years later, I attended a Memorial Meeting at Friends House in London for Gwen Catchpool, who with her husband Corder continued the Quaker relief work in Berlin after the Nazis came to power. The Catchpools helped countless persecuted people to escape from Germany.

During the Meeting of Thanksgiving, one after another of these survivors told touching stories of the way the Catchpools had saved their lives and what the concern of Friends had meant to them in their suffering. Toward the close, an elderly woman rose and gave her name. I was stunned. This was Gerhard's sister!

She spoke with deep emotion of her experiences in the 1930s and expressed gratitude for the help she had been given, both in getting out of Germany and on her arrival in England. The recollection seemed to render her distraught.

When the moving meeting closed, I rushed over to this woman and explained that I had known her mother and her brother in Freiburg.

"You knew my mother?" she cried, incredulous. "You knew my brother?"

Afraid she was going to break down, I nevertheless inquired about Gerhard. She told me that her whole family had been so opposed to the National Socialist Party that when Hitler came to power, they had had to flee. Then Gerhard took part in the unsuccessful plot to assassinate Hitler and narrowly escaped to South America. He had since died.

Sperli the Clockmaker had been well thought out. I knew the language of the country I wrote about and stayed there for six months. But when I planned my third book, I made a bad error in judgment.

The summer before Ellen was born, we spent a month in Visby on the Island of Gotland, which lies in the Baltic Sea, off the coast of Sweden. The town is full of eleventh-century ruins. They were covered with roses when we were there.

Visby appealed to me as a good subject for a children's book. It was beautiful and historically interesting. The clear air, blowing freshly off the Baltic, gave everything a poetical ambience. Dick took up painting.

Why I thought American children would care about eleventh-century ruins or their history, I can't imagine. But I collected a great deal of folklore in Swedish, which I couldn't read. I bought a dictionary.

In the month we spent on the island, there wasn't time to begin writing. I planned to do that when we returned to Baltimore. It was years before I learned that I must never attempt to write about a culture that I don't know intimately, particularly after I've left the country.

A graduate student at Johns Hopkins translated the Swedish books I had brought back. Still, I couldn't get a handle on the writing. What had seemed charming when we were in Visby seemed uninteresting when I recollected it in our sooty Baltimore apartment.

Ellen was born in December 1929. What joy! But I was told that it would not be advisable for me to have another baby.

By the time Dick graduated, he had decided to specialize in pathology. Yale awarded him a fellowship.

We rented a house above Lake Whitney in Hamden, Connecticut. I was much happier in New England, but no more inspired by the Visby material.

Henry Seidel Canby, who had launched me with those reviews, lived across the Lake. His wife was editing the juvenile section of the *Saturday Review* and she sent me several books to review.

I gave up on Visby. What seemed like a much better subject came to me—a life of the child Mozart for children. The Yale Music Library was at my disposal. My enthusiasm returned. I loved doing that story. It was never published. My granddaughter Nancy has the manuscript.

As Ellen turned into a toddler, I realized that I had to make a definite choice—either I must get someone to take care of her for a few hours a day or give up writing. It wasn't only a question of dividing my time. Writing preoccupies me. It was robbing me of the full enjoyment of what I had been told would be my only child. And so I gave up writing.

I had my hands full, anyway. We were on the move again. Dick's fellowship was running out. It was the depth of the Depression. We believed we could live more cheaply that summer in Switzerland.

We found a little chalet in Villars, a village above the Rhone Valley, and loved being there. At the end of the summer, we discovered that the rent for the whole winter was no more than we had been paying for three months. Dick had no prospect of an appointment at home. We stayed a year.

Villars was full of boarding schools and homes for delicate children, who lay out in the sun on cots. It had not yet become a ski resort.

Dick was getting interested in psychiatry. The Swiss National Library sent him books and he studied, sitting on our little terrace under the Dents du Midi.

The chalet was too small for a piano. We found a clavichord in Zurich. I played and played. And I knitted. I learned to ski. But I didn't write.

One day, when we went down into the valley to shop, Ellen and I met Romain Rolland. Ellen was going on three, a most charming and beautiful little girl. She captivated the author. Since first meeting him in Gurnigel, I had become an author, too, with two juveniles to my credit. And yet, the whole time we were in Switzerland, I never wrote.

I did, however, do one thing while we were in Villars that turned out to be more important than anything else I might have done and has brought me the most inestimable joy ever since. I consulted a doctor in Zurich about the possibility of having another child. He assured me that if I took good care of myself for six months, the risk would be small. Thanks to his advice, our lives became enriched by John Nicholas.

Dick decided that he definitely wished to specialize in psychiatry. He secured an appointment in the big mental hospital in Zurich. We found an apartment in Zollikon.

Six months later, we went to England. While Dick worked in a London hospital, Ellen and I played in Kensington Gardens, visiting Peter Pan, who had been honored with a statue by then.

One Sunday, we went to the Meeting for Worship at Friends House in Euston Road. It was our first contact with Friends. I had no idea what to expect. Looking back, I don't recall any of the vocal ministry. It didn't impress me. Nevertheless, that was what Friends call a "gathered" meeting—there was the sense of the presence of God as I had never experienced it in any place of worship. When we left that morning, I knew that I had found what I'd been looking for all my life.

We returned to New Haven in the summer of 1934. Nicky was born the following March.

Apart from one or two short stories, which were not published, I didn't write while the children were small. The way it looked to me then, my career had ended when I was twenty-five. I devoted myself to my family and joined the New Haven Friends Meeting. Life was altogether satisfying.

Learning about Quaker tradition, I discovered a whole body of inspiring literature—the writings of early Friends: George Fox, Isaac Penington, Francis Howgill, and, that lovable master of eighteenth-century English prose, John Woolman.

What George Fox wrote about his climb up Pendle Hill in 1652 intrigued me: "When I was come to the top, I saw the sea bordering on Lancashire." He must have been looking in the direction of my birthplace.

9

When we built our house in Hamden in 1938, we put in a study for Dick, which opened onto the upstairs deck. It has a diminutive fireplace and a window seat with a magnificent view of Lake Whitney and East Rock. Dick actually had very little use for the study because he spent all day in his office at the hospital.

It never occurred to anyone, least of all to me, that I ought to have a room of my own, too. What for? I wasn't a writer any more. Didn't I have the whole kitchen and half a bedroom? What more did I need?

I was happy driving the children to school and to music lessons, running the household, and rolling bandages with the faculty wives. This was what one expected of a married woman in my circumstances.

After the Second World War started and the Germans bombed England, we had a couple of extra children. The faculty of Yale University cabled to the faculties of Oxford and Cambridge, offering to take their children for the duration of the war.

One hundred and forty of these young refugees came to New Haven. We took them into our child-centered families, taught them our habits, helped them to get along in our schools. We loved them and they became attached to us.

But I had had an English childhood, too, even if it was a generation earlier. I thought I knew how different life in the States was for those children. We treated them like our own—honored their preference in the selection of clothes, of what they would like to do. We encouraged them to make all the choices we assume children have the right to make in our comfortable and permissive society.

What would it be like for them if they were able to go home when the war ended? Were we Americanizing them, unfitting them for life in England with their parents, who were fighting for their very existence? If England survived, would these children, who had spent years with us, be capable of adjusting to postwar austerity?

Alastair came to us first. His mother had brought him and his sisters from Oxford. Now she was going back. At the moment, there was no foster home available that was large enough to accommodate all those children, so they were temporarily left in different families. Alastair was six, like Nicky, and also in the first grade at the Foote School. He was a lively, affectionate little boy who fitted right into our family.

What I remember especially is the weekend in December when we all went to our little old farmhouse in Putney, Vermont, to cut the Christmas tree.

Alastair took to Putney as though he'd been born in those hills. He loved the brook and the hayloft and he loved us with that eager, pathetic affection displaced children often reveal. But he never quite came to love Twinkle, our neighbor's cow, which grazed in our pasture.

That Sunday morning, when I came down, I found that the children had done an especially good job of filling the woodbox and so I made pancakes. Ellen, who was twelve, discovered at the back of the cupboard some maple syrup we had made in Easter vacation. Breakfast was a feast. While we lingered at the kitchen table, two fawns came loping along, heavenly creatures whose upturned faces gazed at us trustingly, as if from a Christmas card.

Later, Dick took the boys to our woodlot, an inaccessible bit of forest. Alastair trudged along in his "gum boots," up to his waist in snow. Dick cut the trees—one big one for all of us and a small private one for each of the little boys. Alastair and Nicky dragged their very own trees out to the station wagon.

On our way home to Hamden that afternoon, just before we reached Brattleboro, Alastair started to cry. At first, he wouldn't say what was the matter. Then he complained of the cold. I reached back to where the children were sprawled with their trees and found that Alastair's hands were as warm as toast. Dick stopped the car and lifted the little guy into the space between us on the front seat. He realized that the cold Alastair complained of wasn't in his hands or feet but in his heart—a little refugee facing the prospect of his first Christmas away from home.

We got back late and tucked the sleepy children into bed, even Ellen, our big one.

When our neighbor saw our lights, she telephoned. "I suppose you've heard the news?"

"No," I answered, still glowing with the happiness of the weekend. "We never bother with the papers in Putney. Is there anything special?"

She didn't answer at once. Then she said in a strained voice, "The Japanese have bombed Pearl Harbor."

Next morning, I got up early to tell the children. I didn't want them to be upset. Ellen and Nicky took the news calmly. "War" meant something dreadful but vague, something that happened to people far away.

But for Alastair it was real. It meant leaving home. Just when he had settled in comfortably with us and had a Christmas tree of his very own, war had overtaken him again. I tried to tell him that America wouldn't be bombed, like England, but I wasn't quite sure of that myself. All I knew was that Dick would want to enlist.

After school that day, Alastair wrote to his mother. It

wasn't easy for him to print out his thoughts, but the letter went something like this:

Dear Mummy are you safe? Is Daddy safe? Are the kittens safe?

Later, Jean, a classmate of Ellen's, came to us. She was the most lovable, harum-scarum, redheaded twelve-year-old. Unlike Alastair, she loved Twinkle, the Putney cow. She always volunteered to pick and shuck the corn and brought in more than anyone could eat. After dinner, she scooped up the corncobs and rushed out to offer them tenderly to Twinkle.

Jean was a joy, though when she came to us from summer camp, I felt obliged to suggest that she take a bath. Hadn't there been washing facilities at camp? Oh, yes. They were required to take a shower every day. But she and her bunkmates found that if you were very careful, you could stand in a corner of the shower without getting wet.

New Haven Hospital needed volunteers. I became a ward secretary—work I disliked and felt especially unsuited for.

"This isn't much of a job," the woman who trained me confided, "but it is a chance to meet a doctor." I already had one and was perfectly satisfied. I only took the job because I thought I ought to be rendering some service.

That Christmas, Dick made me a present of something I'd never been given before—money, lots of money. A hundred dollars! He said, "Spend this on something you really want. Don't be practical. Get something you wouldn't otherwise get yourself."

I had everything. I couldn't think of anything I would like to go out and buy. And so this money became a symbol of what I most wanted in life. I thought about it for months.

Finally I decided that what I really wished for was to be

able to write. Now that the children were in school all day, I might spend the money on a course in short story writing. Short pieces would be about all I had time for and I felt ready to write for adults.

There was no course open to me in New Haven. I would have to commute to Columbia.

Ware, one of my college classmates, had become a very successful magazine writer. I asked what she thought about such a course. She said, "Daisy, you know that the only way to learn to write is to write. Don't take a course. Save your money."

I still have it.

Then Ware said, "Besides, you'll never be a short story writer. You're too slow. You ought to be a novelist."

I exclaimed, "Me, a novelist?" I don't know why, but it seemed presumptuous.

I decided to write a novel simply as an exercise—to learn how to put one together. What about? Something I knew at firsthand, something I cared about deeply.

The dilemma of those English children, who, it seemed to me, became less capable of living at home the longer they lived with us, moved me.

I gave up the volunteer job. I was going to write, but only when everyone was in school or at work. Even after I discovered to my great surprise that my books could make money, I still thought of writing as an indulgence that ought never to infringe on my time with Dick and the children.

Now that my consciousness has been raised to the point where I recognize how unfair this assumption was, I'm glad that I was part of my generation and didn't feel abused. Writing created no conflict for me. Those novels reflected my overflowing joy in my family and I think that that is one reason they had so much appeal.

Dick laid a board between the top of the radiator and the filing cabinet in a corner of our bedroom. With my father's old portable on it, this was my work space. I can't remember feeling resentment because I had to make do with the meager arrangement. It would have been unjustified, for, in the next ten years, I produced three successful novels on that board.

I started inventing characters who were not in the least like the children who stayed with us, except that they were in the same predicament and equally lovable. Wincy, thirteen, and Angus, nine, had been evacuated from Oxford, England, to Belmont, Massachusetts. Suppose their parents just happened to be extreme opposites of their foster parents—elderly, anxious, formal, on the one hand; young, modern, and comparatively carefree on the other. Children exposed to such extremes would feel bewildered. Wincy and Angus must be equal to this.

Homecoming, I decided to call my first novel. Where should it start? With their coming home to Oxford, of course. Their life in America could be described in flashbacks.

I wasn't, however, the one who was running this show. To my amazement, I soon discovered that the characters were. As soon as Wincy and Angus stepped off the train in the Oxford station and met their parents, the action started of itself. This was to be my experience with every book and it never ceased to astonish me.

Due to cultural differences, Wincy and Angus got into one tight spot after another, both pathetic and amusing. By the end of the book, they would make a satisfactory adjustment in Oxford, having been enriched rather than alienated by their years in the States.

They returned home in the spring. A much more fitting title suggested itself: *Now That April's There.*

The book is dedicated to Ellen and John Nicholas.

At the end, I had to hurry because Dick had enlisted in the navy. The children and I were planning to go with him until he went overseas.

10

Dick had orders for the Naval Hospital in Bethesda, Maryland. We closed our house in Hamden. All four of us were going with him. When Ellen's winter vacation was over, she would return to boarding school in Vermont. Nicky and I would stay with Dick as long as we could.

What was going to become of Angus and Wincy, while we were away? I couldn't bear to think of them staying behind in the empty house. Had they taught me how to write a novel? Who could tell me?

My friend Ware offered to give the manuscript to her literary agent. He would know whether the book showed promise. If he thought so, he might even submit it to a publisher.

That was more than I considered possible, even more than I dared hope for.

When Dick reported for duty in Bethesda, he was told that he would be sent overseas in three weeks. However, at the end of that time, he got orders for the Naval Hospital in Portsmouth, Virginia.

I wasn't cut out for the military and I suffered for the men in those hospitals. In Portsmouth, we had trouble finding a place to live. Ellen had gone back to school, but none of the landladies would rent to a couple with a nine-year-old boy. Such a dear, reasonable, nondestructive boy!

Having no place to live, Nicky and I went home when Ellen's school closed for the summer. Without the encumbrance of a family, Dick found a room and bath opposite the hospital.

At the end of the summer, friends in Cambridge offered to keep Nicky. Shady Hill School took him in.

Returning to Portsmouth without Nicky, I felt bereft.

A few weeks later, we thought we had a place so I went and got Nicky. By the time we reached Portsmouth, the place had been taken. The owners of the room Dick was staying in were kind enough to let us stay with him. I cooked on a hot plate in the bathroom. Three footlockers made a tolerable bed for Nicky until he got strep throat. A child with fever, it seemed to me, deserved a proper bed.

The war was getting more intense. Every day, I feared that Dick would be sent overseas.

Against this grim background, something wonderful happened.

With all the travelling I'd done, I'd never had an inner landscape, that imaginary place a novelist inhabits quite apart from any actual place. There, in Tidewater, Virginia, I found myself dreaming about a little town near the ocean in Rhode Island. I'd only been there once, for a weekend, a couple of years earlier.

In 1942, New Haven Friends Meeting had sent me as a representative to the little Yearly Meeting of Wilburite Friends, which was being held in Westerly, Rhode Island.

Walking from the railroad station, I was charmed by the town. It still had its magnificent elms. The little dove-gray meetinghouse looked welcoming in the setting sun. Inside, the Friends who had already arrived prayed silently for guidance.

Almost a century earlier, Friends in New England had disagreed so drastically that they separated into two Yearly Meetings. "The Wilburites" and "the Gurneyites," they called themselves. It was a bitter estrangement. The present gener-ation, regretting the events of the past, longed to effect a reunion. The two groups had been separated so long that they thought and worshipped in different manners. Could their longing for reconciliation and the leading of the Spirit help them to reach an overarching unity? There were practical difficulties, too, such as property and bequests, which made any change seem impossible.

It was in the hope of overcoming these difficulties that the Wilburites had invited representatives from the Gurneyite Yearly Meeting and the independent Meetings, like mine, to attend their Yearly Meeting session. That week-end, after much prayerful consideration, "way opened," as Friends say, and three years later, on the one hundredth anniversary of the Separation, all Friends in New England were joyfully gathered into a single Yearly Meeting.

I returned home from Westerly unaware that what I had witnessed during the weekend would influence my writing for the rest of my life.

Now, against the fear and hurt of the war that had reached out and touched our family, I thought longingly of Westerly. It wasn't the actual town that I dreamed of, there in Virginia, but the feeling I'd had as I observed Friends reaching out to one another in love, healing the dissension of a century. It was this recollection of the Spirit bestowing healing peace that brought me comfort in the midst of the war.

Had I not been appointed to take part in those first reconciling efforts, I might never have gone to Westerly and my inner landscape wouldn't have presented itself so comfortingly in Virginia.

Then came the most incredible news. *Now That April's There,* which I had written purely as an exercise, had not only found a publisher, it turned out to be a best-seller. The first chapter appeared in the *New Yorker.* The book was condensed in the *Ladies Home Journal* and selected by a leading book club.

Metro-Goldwin-Mayer acquired the film rights for a very

young actress. I had never heard of her, but it was explained to me that she was thirteen, like my heroine, and that she had made one picture: *National Velvet.* It was Elizabeth Taylor.

The producer came east. I flew to New York. He asked whether I'd come to Hollywood when the film was being made. The sum the agent mentioned as my weekly remuneration was only a little less than I later received from Radcliffe College for a whole academic year's work.

But I refused. If I were to go, who would take care of Nicky? Besides, Dick might be shipped out while I was on the West Coast and I mightn't be able to get back in time to see him once more.

Hollywood impressed people. They might never have read the book. But the movies! The local newspaper wrote me up and printed my picture. I knew I had arrived when Dick's commanding officer's wife asked me to buy some meat for her. It was scarce and the butcher played favorites. After that article appeared in the paper, I could have had anything.

None of this went to my head. I discovered that success can bring sorrow, too.

Naturally, my mother was pleased. But I regretted that my father couldn't have lived to witness my good fortune. When I was writing those first stories and making those little books, he was so baffled, even worried. I was wasting my time on childish, impractical things. Would I ever grow up?

What hurt most was a subtle change in attitude that I sensed on the part of some of my friends when I went home. They had always thought of me as just a nice housewife, except that I scribbled for a hobby. Those children's books I had published posed no threat to their egos. But now that I had a best-seller and was making a lot of money, they didn't like me quite so much. Somehow, they felt I had betrayed them. It isn't only adversity that teaches you who your friends are; success does that, too.

Dick got orders to return to Bethesda. While we were there, Elizabeth Taylor came to Washington to speak from the White House for the March of Dimes. Mrs. Taylor invited me to come and meet Elizabeth. *Now that April's There* was to be her next picture.

She was beautiful, just a spontaneous little girl, running up and down the corridors of the Shoreham Hotel, giving the elevator operators her autograph. Her mother kept fussing at her to eat her lettuce, telling me that she wanted Elizabeth to grow up like any normal girl.

The film script was sent back and forth across the ocean to ensure that all the details were accurate. Because of the war, it took ages. By the time the script was ready, Elizabeth had grown up. Overnight, she turned into a woman who bore no relation to my innocent heroine. So the film was never made.

But I got the money. For the first time in my life, I owned more than a couple of thousand dollars. Some I gave away. The rest I hoarded, indifferent, because I had no use for it. What could I possibly want?

Fortunately, I had no means of knowing that in a decade my life would be completely changed; that I would be alone, unable to maintain my big house, and that, thanks to this money, I could build a dear little one on my land.

11

Having had this unexpected success with my first novel, I thought I just might get away with writing about an unpopular character—a conscientious objector. In wartime! There was no peace movement in that war. If you weren't for it, you were practically a traitor. And there I was, attached by marriage to the armed forces.

Many, though by no means all, Quaker men of draft age wished to be classified as conscientious objectors on religious grounds. If their request was granted, they were assigned to Civilian Public Service camps, which the government asked the American Friends Service Committee to supervise. In the camps, the men were to be engaged in meaningful service.

I knew some of these C.O.s and sympathized with their quandary. They were convinced that it was wrong to kill. But they also felt guilty. Equally sincere men were willing to die so that they might be free to obey their consciences. If I could communicate the mixed feelings of the conscientious objectors, those who condemned them as cowards might be more understanding.

I could appreciate both sides. I was a Friend. I was also observing daily the suffering the men in the Naval Hospital endured.

I thought I could identify with the ambivalence of my hero, could feel myself inside his skin. Bart, I called him. He was just a nice, ordinary young man, thrust into an intolerable situation by his Quaker heritage. What would be the means of confirming him in his pacifist position, of assuaging his pain?

Only a deep experience of worship with Friends, as I

myself had known it at Yearly Meeting in Westerly, would have the power to reenforce him.

This, then, would be a Quaker novel, an attempt to show the mystical experience that led Friends to accept their Peace Testimony, unpopular and costly though it was.

A Quaker novel? Wasn't that a contradiction in terms? The early Friends called themselves Publishers of Truth. Could a Friend also be a publisher of fiction? What is a novelist but one who constructs a pack of lies?

The *Discipline* of New England Yearly Meeting, published in 1809, stated: "It is earnestly recommended to every member of our religious society that they discourage and suppress the reading of plays, pernicious novels, or other bad books." And as late as 1874, when the Friends Free Library of Germantown was opened, the Alfred Cope Book Trust, which provided funds, stipulated that "works of fictitious character, commonly called novels," were to be excluded.

Nowadays, most Friends tolerate "novels and other bad books," which is fortunate, because for me the two vocations—the publishing of Truth and the publishing of fiction—are so integrated that I don't know where my religious experience leaves off and my literary inspiration begins.

Novels are about people, their inner lives as well as their actions. And it's the people I've worshipped and worked with on concerns over the past fifty years who have given depth to my writing.

At their finest, these Friends radiated a rare serenity. They were fun to be with, too—full of humor, which I interpreted as a measure of their humility. They took their religion very seriously but they never took themselves too seriously. Even their foibles, which could be maddening, were a little endearing, a reminder that the most spiritual of Friends are, like the rest of us, all too human.

Thinking of them, I found the verse from Genesis echoing in my head: There were giants in the earth in those days. Quaker giants!

Many of them were eminent scholars. Fifty years ago, that meant they were mostly men. Here I was—young, ignorant, and a woman—and these weighty Friends accorded me the same affectionate respect they gave each other. I wasn't used to that in the world outside. It made me more aware of "that of God" in me. It gave me confidence.

And if Quaker women of my generation aren't such assertive feminists as our younger sisters would like us to be, that's why. In the Society of Friends, we had equality. We didn't have to fight for it. Quaker men made us feel our worth.

In the novel about a conscientious objector, which I planned to write, these types would be the supporting characters.

I wanted to lay the action in my inner landscape and thought of going back to Westerly some day to reawaken the feeling I had had there on my first visit.

But I was afraid. I didn't know those Friends. They might resent having their meetinghouse populated with fictional characters who had experiences in it that never took place there. Or they might quite simply try to advise me how to write my book. If I went to Westerly, I could lose my independence. Fears like these haunted me before I knew those Friends.

So I decided on Nantucket, which is rich in Quaker history. As far as I knew, there were no year-round Friends living there then. Nantucket would be safe.

The children and I spent that summer in Woods Hole on

Cape Cod. From there I sailed over to Nantucket on the ferry, hoping to discover a background against which my characters would come to life. As I walked up from the dock to the center of town and took in the beauty and simplicity of the old brick houses, I was sure that would happen.

At one time, there were thousands of Friends on Nantucket. Then, due partly to their bickering over "plainness"—they used to go to one another's houses and if they found fringes on the antimacassars, they snipped them off—and partly to the decline of the whaling industry, many of them migrated to the mainland. By 1900, the only Friends on Nantucket were summer visitors. Much later, George and Florence Selleck retired there, but, in the Forties, there was no Quaker presence.

The librarians and the curator in the museum were very interested in my project. They showed me dozens of Quaker bonnets and books of genealogy.

"My grandmother was a Friend," they would tell me. "But she married out." Or they would say, "I trace my ancestry clear back to Mary Starbuck, the first Islander to become a Quaker. But my family has belonged to the Unitarian Church for generations." None of this gave me the sense of immediate reality that I needed. What was wrong?

I returned to Woods Hole no more inspired than before.

At the end of August, Ellen went back to boarding school and Nicky and I returned to Bethesda. Several times a week, I travelled to the Library of Congress, trying to learn more about the history of Nantucket Friends.

Suddenly, one day I woke up to what should have been an obvious fact from the beginning—I could never lay the action of a contemporary Quaker novel in Nantucket precisely because there were no Friends there. Quaker worship was a living experience, not embalmed in history. I needed the companionship of other seekers to be able to communicate something authentic.

And so I threw all my Nantucket notes away and wrote to Henry Perry, the clerk of New England Yearly Meeting, in whom I felt free to confide. I asked him whether he thought I dared go to Westerly.

He wrote back, "My cousins Phebe and Thomas are coming from Westerly next week to attend a meeting of the American Friends Service Committee. I'll ask them how they would feel about being placed in a fishbowl."

Fishbowl! That was not at all what I had in mind.

The following week I had a letter from Westerly. Phebe Perry was inviting us to visit her as soon as the war was over. It seemed a long time to wait.

Dick never was sent overseas. In June of 1946, when the war was finally over, we went home, trailing a little sailboat he had acquired in Portsmouth.

The first thing we did after we got to Hamden was to go to see Ellen. Then, leaving Nicky with friends, we went to Westerly for the weekend.

On the drive over, I was nervous. Would those Friends understand that I didn't intend to "put them in a fishbowl?" Would they realize that I wasn't a reporter or a social scientist, that my characters are paper people, with personalities of their own, not portraits of people I've actually known, and that my inner landscape isn't their town but only the feeling I had sitting in their meetinghouse years earlier?

Phebe Perry was a beautiful woman, active in Quaker and community affairs. Although she was unmarried, she had a family of adopted children. Her brother Thomas lived next door. When Dick and I arrived, they took us riding along the shore. They showed us the old Quaker burial ground. Then they brought us to the home of their brother Harvey and his wife. Their house overlooked a salt pond, separated from the ocean by sand dunes.

Twenty-six years later, this land- and seascape would become the inspiration for Firbank in *I Take Thee, Serenity* and, later yet, in *Indian Summer of the Heart.* When that time came, it would be Thomas's son Tom who would take me over the terrain, teaching me about the birds and the vegetation and the little creatures on the edge of the pond. But all this was far in the future.

When Dick and I went up to Phebe's guest room the night of our first visit, he said to me, "You were wrong to be afraid of these Friends. They're in character. You're going to have a lovely time here."

And I did. My inner landscape was confirmed. I called it Kendal, after the town in the north of England where Quakerism first took hold.

A year later, the story of the conscientious objector was finished. The working title had been *Take Nothing for Your Journey,* quoted from the ninth chapter of the Gospel of Luke. But as the story progressed, Thoreau's *Walden* furnished a more fitting title: *A Different Drummer.*

Thomas and Phebe and I read the manuscript aloud one memorable weekend. They were very pleased.

I had vowed to myself that I wouldn't publish anything about Friends that didn't have the approval of Henry Cadbury. Chairman of the American Friends Service Committee, Hollis Professor of Divinity at Harvard, one of the editors of the Revised Standard Version of the Bible, Henry was, above all, a beloved friend and preceptor to many of us. So I sent him a copy of the manuscript. To the end, he liked to say that this was my best book.

But the publishers didn't think so. No one would touch it. "Too hot to handle," they called it; they'd get thousands of protests from people whose sons had gone to war.

From having had such unexpected success, I had a complete failure. It seemed worse because the Westerly Friends had been so hospitable. But they never let me feel that they were disappointed in me.

I was. If I had been more skillful and experienced, I told myself, I might have succeeded. Second novels are notoriously troublesome. Why did I think that I was capable of writing convincingly about a young man? What did I really know about how he felt? I must never again try to write from the masculine point of view.

This book failed to find a publisher, but it was far from a failure. Very soon I would discover that it was going to determine the tenor of my writing throughout my career.

First and foremost, it brought me the friendship of those who entertained me. I had come simply to write about their world. In no time, I found that I had acquired real friends. By their love and example, by their warmth and openness and absolute integrity, they strengthened my resolve to do my best.

A Different Drummer hadn't really been a failure. With it, I simply served my apprenticeship.

In due time, the mystical experience I longed to communicate would flower in the four Kendal novels. Then, letters from unknown readers would show that something of the beautiful spirit of these dear Friends still lived. Long after they ceased to grace their hometown, they would be vibrantly alive in Kendal; they would inspire and uplift not only those who had once known them but many more who never had the good fortune.

12

What would happen, I asked myself, if a hard-boiled New York businesswoman were to come to Kendal by chance and meet Friends like these?

It had occurred to me that there might be another way of communicating the Quaker experience. Instead of showing it through the eyes of a character like Bart, who is inside the Society, looking out, I would describe the effect on someone who is outside, looking in.

I could already see her, dressed to kill, stepping off the train in the little Kendal station, unaware that she is entering a world with a totally different value system.

Her name is Vaughn Hill. She's really a nice person and basically honest but terribly ambitious, so intent on getting ahead in an advertising agency that she isn't always particular about the way she does it. She puts so much of herself into her work that there's very little left over for her husband and children, who need her more than she knows.

She's making a layout for a railroad account and thinks it would be dramatic to drag in the Underground Railroad, though she doesn't know anything about that. At the library on Forty-second Street she discovers that there is still evidence of a hiding place for runaway slaves in a little town in Rhode Island called Kendal. She's never heard of it but she writes there to ask if she may come to see the hiding place the following weekend and gets a reply from someone named Philip Ludlow. He tells her she's welcome to come.

So that's where Vaughn lands one weekend, right amongst Friends.

Suppose Philip Ludlow, the elderly Friend who meets

the New York train and takes her to his house for dinner, instead of dropping her at a hotel, as she'd expected, has the unaffected goodness, the humor and charm of Thomas Perry and the woman at whose house Vaughn is invited to spend the night is as gracious as his sister Phebe. What would happen?

Suppose Vaughn goes to meeting that Sunday. It's the last thing she wants to do. Religion isn't her thing. She's more concerned with her appearance—her clothes and the impression she makes on people. But these Quakers have treated her as if she were a personal friend, not someone who has come strictly for business. Philip Ludlow has been so kind that when he asks her to go to meeting with him she feels it would be discourteous to refuse. Besides, she likes being with him. So there she sits in the strange silence of the meetinghouse with nothing to do but think about her life. That makes her miserable.

Going to Kendal might change her life, not alone hers but her family's, as well. In Kendal she might discover that one sometimes has to work at loving, too.

So *Diligence in Love* took shape.

When we were in England years earlier—1937—Dick had picked up a copy of Jevons's *Logic*. In it was part of a sonnet that we both liked:

> He who metes, as we should mete,
>   Could we His insight use, shall most approve,
>   Not that which fills most space in earthly eyes,
>   But what—though Time scarce note it as he flies—
>   Fills, like this little daisy at my feet,
>   Its function best of diligence in love.

I had used the title before. In 1937, the Spanish civil war was raging. Near Southampton we saw a tent encampment where nuns were caring for masses of Basque children, who had been evacuated to England. Touched with pity, I later wrote a short story about a young woman in a tiny village in Hampshire who takes in one of these children. Six years old, he is suffering from shock. The young woman's diligence in love slowly brings the boy back to health.

That story, one of the few that I wrote at the time, was not accepted for publication. And so, fourteen years later, I used the title again, this time with great success. Quoting the poem at the front of the book, I acknowledged the source. It seemed to me that I ought to take the reader into my confidence about Kendal, too. So I wrote this note:

> Kendal is not quite an imaginary place, though one may cover the whole of Rhode Island without seeing it. Philip Ludlow and the others there are not quite imaginary people, though—unlike Vaughn who is wholly fictitious—one may not be able to take a train at Grand Central and find them. They live, not in the flesh, but in the aspiration of those who cherish a particular way of life.
>
> The key to the Meetinghouse hangs on a nail in the south wall, above the syringa bush. Anyone may open the door.

The key actually did hang on the outside wall of the Westerly Meetinghouse then. Those Friends were completely trusting. Later, boys from the neighborhood let themselves in to smoke unobserved and Friends worried about fire. They decided that a member who lived across the street had better keep the key at her house. But when I was writing the book, it hung outside so that anyone—a passing stranger, perhaps—might enter the meetinghouse to rest and center down.

It was fun watching Vaughn mature as the story unfolded and she came to see that reality was more important than appearance. Denny, her husband, and Neil and Susan, their children, come into their own as Vaughn gains insight. The whole family ends up in Kendal, liberated to begin leading the kind of lives they really want.

Bart, the conscientious objector, quite naturally walked into this book. Seen through Vaughn's eyes, he is much more believable than he was in *A Different Drummer.*

Naomi, who represented me at the literary agency, placed the book with Doubleday. When I delivered the finished manuscript, the editor showed me the design for the jacket. It portrayed a woman, presumably Vaughn, walking toward a little frame building that was meant to be a Quaker meetinghouse. But the windows of the building all had Gothic points! I explained to the editor that these were unacceptable. She couldn't see why the points made any difference.

"People died in defense of the right to worship in buildings without those points!" I cried. "They believed one can worship God anywhere, not just in a church."

Eventually, the jacket design was changed, but the advertisement in the *New York Times Book Review* carried the original Gothic windows.

I realized then that I needed to explain more about peculiar Quaker language: that Friends originally called themselves "Friends of the Truth" or "Publishers of Truth" but that an angry judge whom they urged to "tremble at the word of the Lord" called them "Quakers" and the term of reproach stuck; that, rather than use pagan names for the days of the week—Sun Day, Moon Day—they numbered them; that many Friends still go to meeting on First Day. And I explained to the bewildered editor that what Friends call a "leading" is an idea that they believe to have been divinely inspired.

On the last day of January 1951, the printer delivered

some advance copies of *Diligence in Love* to the Doubleday office. I went down to New York to pick one up so I'd have it to bring to Thomas the next day, his seventy-first birthday.

When I presented the book to him, I opened it to the dedication, which I knew he would recognize as being in part a quotation from George Fox:

> To one who walks cheerfully over the world.

And I explained that Thomas was that one. The book was dedicated to him.

He said nothing till he had read it. Then he observed with his usual modesty, "It has nothing to do with me. It's about an ideal person."

I didn't try to convince him. But I wished he could see himself in Philip Ludlow and realize how much he communicated to others of the good and the beautiful.

He must have felt this more than he admitted because, three days later, he wrote to me:

> May I say what hardly needs saying—that there isn't a thing about *Diligence* and hasn't been from beginning to end that hasn't seemed to me perfectly conceived and executed. It has been a joy to see it take shape and be born.

When I next saw him and we were speaking about the book, he murmured diffidently, "It's a kind of immortality."

After *Diligence in Love* appeared, I was asked for the first time to speak to a Friends meeting.

"Who?" I felt like writing back to Philadelphia, "Me?" I was scared pink.

The train was late. A Friend I didn't know met me. He took me to the home of someone who was giving a dinner party in honor of the evening's speaker. I was introduced to a bunch of weighty Friends. I figured they'd been impatient for my arrival so they could start to eat. By the time we entered the large, elegantly appointed dining room, I felt like crawling under the table. Instead, I was seated beside the hostess.

After the silent grace, there was a lot of conversation while a waitress went around serving crackers. When she came to me, she served me from the wrong side. I figured she was inexperienced help, brought in for the evening. Later, I realized that she'd been instructed to do this.

The hostess picked up her soup spoon. All conversation ceased and all eyes seemed to be on me. I picked up my soup spoon. The hostess laid hers down and, turning to me, declared, "I knew you were left-handed!"

Everyone roared. Except, of course, the guest of honor.

How did the hostess know? She'd never laid eyes on me till ten minutes ago. And why was she making such a big thing about it? I felt the way I had in that French school the year I was seven. Later, one of the guests told me that before I arrived, our hostess had talked of nothing else, so sure was she that her surmise was correct.

As we were leaving for the meetinghouse where I, far from calm, was scheduled to speak, I asked the hostess how she knew I was left-handed.

"You wrote," she explained, "that the first time Vaughn went to meeting, she put a fifty-cent piece in her glove for the collection plate, not knowing that the Kendal Friends didn't pass one. She forgets about the coin till Philip Ludlow shakes hands with her at the close of meeting. Then she feels this hard thing pressing into her palm."

The hostess scanned my face to see whether I'd caught on yet. But I was dense. "Only a left-handed person could have written that," she pointed out. "A right-handed person would have had Vaughn put the money in her left glove."

It was a lesson. Since then I've been more careful about accuracy.

I got through that first talk to Philadelphia Friends only

because Mary Hoxie Jones and Sylvia and Harold Evans had come and I felt reassured, seeing some familiar faces in the audience.

Letters from unknown readers started coming. They wrote from all parts of the country. I had been thinking of myself as an ivory tower person, writing in my lovely home above Lake Whitney. And yet, something reached distant people with whom I would have thought I had little in common. It was, of course, the Quaker way of life and the beautiful quotations in the book that moved them.

A woman in the West wrote, "Life was so awful, I had to do something." In desperation, she did what was apparently extraordinary for her. "I decided," she wrote, "to read a book. I went to the library and the librarian suggested yours." She went on to say what it had done for her.

I felt both gratified and humbled.

After the book appeared in England, the BBC did a series of daily readings. The father of Alastair, the boy who had been with us for a while during the war, had recordings made of these readings and sent them to me.

One day I received a big wad of newspaper clippings, which turned out to be in Dutch. *Volharding in de Liefde, Dagelijks feuilleton door Daisy Newman,* each of the eighty-two clippings was entitled. I figured these were daily intallments of *Diligence in Love.* But no one had told me about the sale of rights in the Netherlands and I hadn't received any royalties. That, my agent explained, when I inquired, was because there was no sale. The book had simply been pirated.

I pasted the clippings in a scrapbook and forgot about them. I knew no one who spoke Dutch.

Twenty years later, Queen Juliana of the Netherlands appointed Irving, my son-in-law, to be a visiting professor at the University of Leyden. In preparation for his year there, Irv looked around Cleveland and found a Dutchman who gave him Dutch lessons. I sent Irv copies of the feuilletons and his teacher put them on tape so Irv could learn the pronunciation. That gave me more pleasure than all the royalties in Holland!

Now, thirty-four years after Doubleday brought out *Diligence in Love* and Hodder and Stoughton published it in England, the Family Bookshelf is reissuing it in America.

I wish Thomas could know that Philip Ludlow is about to interpret his way of life to a whole new generation, one that is hungering to read about gentle spirits such as his.

"It's a kind of immortality."

13

"Is Kendal a real place?" readers ask when they write, meaning, I suppose, Can they go there? And I have to reply that it isn't a place they can drive or fly to or go to by train. But, I assure them, they don't need transportation. They're already there.

Kendal is a real place if that's where they go when they feel jaded or defeated and need to be reminded that their lives hold endless promise, that there's a spark of the divine, not only in others but in themselves, too. It's real if they reach for the key that's hanging on the south wall above the syringa bush, let themselves into the quiet meetinghouse, and discover that they aren't alone. For they'll be welcomed by Philip Ludlow or Dilly Fuller or Oliver and Daphne Otis or Serenity and Peter Holland or Loveday Mead or any of the others who are now their treasured friends.

And after they've centered down for a while, when they turn to clasp the hand of the person next to them, they'll find they have hold of that transcendent self they were afraid they'd lost.

I never dreamed, after *Diligence in Love* was finished, that a whole series of novels located in Kendal would follow. But, like those readers who write to me, I need to go home to Kendal sometimes, too. So when I decided to write *The Autumn's Brightness,* that's where I started.

Dilly Fuller, a middle-aged widow, does the reverse of what Vaughn did. She travels from Kendal to New York. There, most unexpectedly, she finds fulfillment.

She had gone to New York to visit her worldly cousin Elmira, whose major interest is the mongrel she calls Henderson. But there was no place for Dilly's tastes and values in

Elmira's apartment, and Dilly was miserable until Durand Smith appeared and took her on an enchanted journey high above the city.

The Third Avenue Elevated was still standing when I wrote the book, but it was already doomed. This is the disclaimer:

Now that the Third Avenue Elevated is being laid off bit by bit, its run curtailed, its schedule cut, there hardly seems any necessity to disclaim living counterparts for Dilly and Durand. Though the structure of the El is still there and its six-car trains operate with the faithfulness of the aging servant, though the crimson windowpanes and potbellied stoves still grace the waiting rooms, the El is nonetheless slipping into the unreality of yesterday. Dilly and Durand travel in that unreality. Indeed, of all the characters, only Henderson aspires to being a likeness. His prototype, compounded of many strains, is everywhere.

Yet, in one respect, even Dilly and Durand are drawn from life. They live in the sensibility of any who may have discovered tender companionship in an unlikely place, at an unlikely time, or who may have known supreme excitement in dividing—with the proper person—a pennyworth of chocolate.

The Sears People's Book Club, which had distributed *Now That April's There* to its members, now selected *The Autumn's Brightness*. The editor asked Ellen and me to write about our family for their publication, *The People's Choice*. Ellen wrote:

Whenever our mother gets a certain eager, far-off look, my brother Nicky and I exchange glances of resigned despair. That look means "Idea for a Book." . . . Once Mother apologized to Nicky for having to meet a deadline during his vacation, saying, "I must be very difficult to have around when I'm writing."

"That's O.K.," he replied magnanimously, "You're worse when you're not."

A slender woman, soft-voiced, with hazel eyes ready to laugh with you, Mother manages to keep a well-ordered house and write, and also to hover over a rose garden, learn to speak Italian— her latest venture!—and, summer weekends, to sail. When it rains, the cook must stand in oilskins, both to keep dry and to be ready to lend a hand on deck if necessary. Priming the stove with four good squirts of alcohol and sending a nervous glance toward the fire extinguisher, Mother turns out mouth-watering swordfish, enormous foamy omelets, and tiny crisp pancakes. . . . Mother doesn't write on the boat. She seems to do this between hanging up the laundry and going to the store. . . . She doesn't even have a special room to write in. Rather, she sits wedged in a narrow corner of the bedroom overlooking the garden, while a cup of tea clatters on the saucer beside her in synchrony with the typewriter keys.

I explained the allusion to the pennyworth of chocolate:

One winter day, while we stood on the El platform, waiting for a train, Dick put two pennies in a slot and drew out two miniature chocolate bars which he broke in halves, offering part of each to me. . . . My pleasure must have shone in my face because ever after that when we stood waiting for a train Dick did the same thing. So, much later, did Durand, making the offering to Dilly that Dick had made to me.

The book was published first by Hodder and Stoughton in England under the title *Dilly*. Shortly afterward, Macmillan brought it out in this country. They had asked me to think up another title. John Greenleaf Whittier, the Quaker poet, furnished it. The American title comes from this line: "The Autumn's brightness after latter rain."

The dedication reads:

For Dick and *Polly*

The little sailboat Dick brought home from Portsmouth had been superceded by *Polly,* a yacht we could cruise in, though she wasn't very big, either. Of her I wrote in *The People's Choice:*

She's my rival. Dick loves *Polly,* too. In fact, though he does well enough by me, it's *Polly* he longs to support in style. My old cord skirt and jacket can easily do another summer. . . . But wouldn't *Polly* look beautiful in a new suit of sail, fine Egyptian cotton or—if we can economize enough on other things— dacron? And maybe, Dick murmurs, gazing fondly at *Polly,* a nylon anchor-line, a bronze winch, stainless steel halyards . . .

We cruise on her in vacation, Dick and the children and I, across Long Island Sound or eastward as far as Maine. She's unbelievably narrow for four. . . . Passing each other we have to pull our stomachs in.

You're no sooner settled in the cockpit than someone decides to have a Coke and you have to get up again because you're sitting on the icebox. The charts are stowed under our mattresses and it seems—this mayn't actually be the case, but it feels as if—charts are always being wanted in the middle of the night.

We have all the harbors rated, Ellen and I, not according to the quality of the holding ground, like our Skipper and Mate, but merely as to conveniences ashore—whether there's a hospitable refuge with plenty of hot water where we can wash our hair. In another few months, though, Ellen will be a doctor. . . . Next summer she'll be an interne in a hospital. And what ever will become of me, without her?

There'll be the whole of the cooking then and I'll still be expected to stand my watch. . . . I'm afraid I do sometimes rush forward to hold onto Nicky's foot while he's shortening sail in a heavy sea. He hopes to design boats after he's finished school and I wish he'd think up some built-in device for mothers, to keep their hearts from sinking when green and white water washes over the rail . . .

What gave me the utmost pleasure was the news that the Division for the Blind of the Library of Congress had awarded a contract to the Braille Institute for the transcription of *The Autumn's Brightness* into Braille.

At Christmas, Hodder and Stoughton sent me a magnificent present: a copy of *Dilly* bound in red morocco leather with sides and endpapers of a beautiful feathery pattern. The title and my name are tooled in gold between raised bands. It's a treasure.

Nevertheless, that was a sad Christmas. Instead of celebrating the birth of love in the world, I mourned the death of a love I had believed to be inviolate. After twenty-eight years, our marriage had come to an end.

I had no way of knowing that this was also a beginning— the climate in which the insight permeating my later novels would be born. Having lost financial security, I took the first job that was offered and gained not only autonomy but a wider vision.

Until then, acute trouble had seemed to be something reserved for others. When our family joined hands around the dinner table to give thanks, an unbroken circle of love, I didn't really know how those others felt. Much of my time was spent helping people in need, out of compassion, not with any perception of what it was like to be inside their skins. A writer must know this.

The time had come for me to learn.

14

What I discovered first was how many people were ready to support me. They seemed to spring up like snowdrops in my garden after the hard winter. "Come and stay with us any time," they said, fifteen of my neighbors and friends.

Their concern touched me. But all I wanted was to stay in my own house, to keep it for the children to come home to.

Home is where I write best and I was in the middle of a novel, not about Kendal. It would have been better if I could have taken refuge there. This was a fantasy about a Yale historian who goes to the Bahamas to locate the Fountain of Youth. Starting out as a rational research project, his quest falls off the edge into unreality.

Home was where I wanted to stay, but I worried about myself. If I spent my days in a fantasy world and never saw anyone in the evening, I might very well become disoriented. So I stood at my door looking up and down the hill and asked myself which of those fifteen homes that I'd been offered would be the most steadying.

My feet answered by crossing Deepwood Drive and following the path to the big yellow house. That was where I would feel most at ease.

Bruce and Rosalind Simonds, my pianist friends, took me into their home each evening and into their loving care. They were deeply religious and that suited my temperament. But all three of us knew that we must never discuss doctrine. We would have disagreed violently. Doctrine wasn't, however, what shone from Bruce and Rosalind, in their faces or their playing. What they communicated was pure spirit.

I had always gone to their public concerts. Now I was privileged to sit by the fire in their studio almost every evening and listen to them play—sometimes both, sometimes just Bruce. Nothing could have been more healing, more uplifting. Each morning I returned home, fortified, and started to write.

Thornton Wilder, also my neighbor, was celebrating his fifty-ninth birthday. His sister Isabel invited me to a party.

Our association went back nearly twenty years. I remembered the Hallowe'en that I went up Deepwood Drive with my children and found Thornton trying to calm his mother after pranksters had stolen her garbage can; the times he invited Ellen, who at twelve was already a good musician, to play Mozart sonatas with him. I could still see her pigtails bobbing as she trudged up the hill, carrying her violin case.

Like Romain Rolland, Thornton was a writer-musician. He was a lively, affectionate, unpretentious man. To be with him was like going to the theater. He talked at top speed, though never rapidly enough to match his zest. His own jokes threw him into gales of laughter. One would have thought he was a small boy.

But I had also seen another side of Thornton at the Edinburgh Festival, where I attended the dress rehearsal and opening night of *The Alcestiad,* the play that seemed to be exceptionally dear to him. He had high hopes for its success until it received destructive reviews and failed to get the Broadway engagement Thornton had counted on. When I saw him a day or two later, he said nothing about this, but I knew. His courageous bearing in the face of disappointment was an example that impressed me deeply at a time when I was struggling to come to terms with the most grievous disappointment of my life.

What could I bring to someone like that in celebration of his birthday? Any tangible gift seemed inappropriate, belittling. Pondering and pondering, I came to the frightening conclusion that the most precious thing I had to give, just then, was the manuscript I was working on. In those days, I never showed work in progress to anyone. Later, I was lucky and found first readers I could trust to be objective, but at the time, the idea of exposing unfinished work to anyone, let alone a craftsman of Thornton's stature, was frightening. I hoped he would understand that my gift was meant as a tribute.

That's what I carried with me when I went to Thornton's birthday party—a xerox copy of *The Fountain of Bimini*. The frontispiece was an antique map of the Bahamas and the title page had a medallion with a portrait of Ponce de Leon. His graying beard shows how old he is and his eyes have the desperate look of all those middle-aged men who set out to find the Fountain of Youth.

I never dreamed that Thornton would care enough to suggest ways that the novel could be improved. Ten days later, I received a letter:

Great charm. Yet all depends on this surprise ending. I'm going to venture to make a suggestion or two. (Don't *take* them; just think them over.)

There were four or five excellent suggestions. How could Thornton have imagined that I wouldn't *take* them? The letter ended:

I could wish that you would hold the book a little longer; there are possibilities of lurking ironies and other meanings. . . . And I think I can guess your ending. Anyway, I have an ending in mind. A penny for my thoughts!

With real thanks and admiration . . .

A few days later, he arrived with a sealed envelope containing his idea for the ending. I wasn't to open it till the book was finished.

To my way of thinking, a novel can only have one ending. The author may set the story up so that the reader envisages several possibilities. That is how the suspense is maintained. But when the reader finishes the book, he or she must be able to look back and see that only this one ending is valid.

If Thornton had a different ending, I must have furnished the wrong clues. I worried. But I didn't peek into the envelope.

Finishing that book took determination. I'd always written from exuberance, the way other women sing around the house. But grief saps creativity. After one has lived through it, grief can be enlarging to an artist. But while it is fresh, grief is debilitating. Still, I persisted.

Finally, the last chapter was written. I tore open Thornton's envelope and read his ending. It was essentially the same as mine! The maestro would have written it as I did. Wasn't that a guarantee of success?

In a later note, Thornton went so far as to predict that the book would be made into a movie.

But, comforting though it was to have his approval, I was forced to recognize that Thornton's enthusiasm was not echoed by the publishers. No one accepted the book.

I needed the money. I was fifty-one, had never held a job, and wasn't qualified for any. Writing was my way of earning and now it failed me.

At that point, Radcliffe College offered me a job for the next academic year as head resident of Holmes Hall, where I would have the care of 102 young women.

A housemother! I was to be a housemother, like Miss Whitney at Barnard Hall the year I was a freshman, only I didn't have a cat.

I would also be director of the Radcliffe College Music Center. The salary for the two jobs was a disgrace. But I'd be given maintenance. I wouldn't have to sell my house. The land my children had played on would still be ours.

I rushed to tell Bruce and Rosalind that I was being engaged to run a concert series. Admission was free. The artists' honoraria would, therefore, be small. Could I secure good artists in spite of this?

Bruce had been dean of the Yale Music School. He said he knew many first-rate musicians who would be grateful for the chance to perform at Radcliffe, even for a small fee.

And so I took the job, knowing that I'd be too busy to write. For the second time in my life, I thought sadly that my writing career was over.

How could I guess that what I was about to experience at Radcliffe would enrich my novels beyond anything I might have learned, had I been allowed to complete my course there as an undergraduate?

15

In September, when I drove up to the locked hall, I was entering into an experience that, far from terminating my writing career, would—if only I might have known it then—enhance my novels as long as I produced them.

All I was aware of at that moment was the fervent hope that I wasn't coming empty-handed, that I'd enrich the lives of those entrusted to my care. It never occurred to me that they'd enrich mine, too.

There wasn't another soul in the huge building. It felt eerie. The living room, large enough to double as a concert hall, looked like a deserted hotel lobby.

Whatever my spirit may or may not have brought, my arms, at least, were full of flowers. On the way up from Hamden, I had spent the night at Phebe's house. Before I left, she stripped her garden for me. My first act was to fill all the vases I could find with gladioli, snapdragons, zinnias, and marigolds, surrounded by fronds of fern. The petunias were charming in a low bowl, which I set on the massive oak table in the living room. Each evening in term time, I would sit at that table and dispense a hundred cups (we had real china in those days) of after-dinner coffee.

The hall already looked less institutional. There was a job I was qualified for, after all—homemaking! Hadn't I had twenty-eight years of experience?

The upperclassmen—upperclasswomen, I should say—moved in the next day, old-timers, going around as if they owned the place. With me they were polite but wary, waiting to see how I compared with my predecessor.

I asked that each of the fifty incoming freshmen and her

parents be brought to my living room as soon as they arrived. I wanted to greet them individually. When the freshmen came in, I wondered whether they guessed that I was as scared and green as they were.

There was a lot to get used to: the peoply smell that permeated the building; 102 voices accompanying the clatter of dishes in the resonant dining room; the paperwork that served no useful purpose; night raids on the kitchen, which was supposed to be locked up. Many of my girls were uncommonly pretty and the watchman was a pushover.

Before breakfast, boys were already on the doorstep. The housemother was supposed to see that they didn't sneak up to the girls" rooms. Now they live in them!

Two weeks after college opened, *Sputnik* was launched. Everyone thought it impressive. No one realized that our world would never be the same.

A week later, my first grandchild was born—James Bartram Newman, named for my father, which made me especially happy, and his maternal grandfather.

I had to share the wonderful news so I ran over to Bates Street, where Amos and Catharine Wilder lived, and they rejoiced with me. Amos had succeeded Henry Cadbury as Hollis Professor of Divinity at Harvard. He and Catharine lived about as far from Holmes as Thornton and Isabel lived from my house in Hamden. "A Wilder in every port," was what their brother Amos said I had. I felt blessed.

Whenever I could get away from the hall for an hour or so, I rushed down Memorial Drive to the M.I.T. graduate student housing, where Nicky and Kathy had secured an apartment. From the first, Jimmy and I had a relationship that has been indescribably precious to me.

I couldn't stay away from Holmes too long. There was so much to do.

In those days, we referred to college students as girls and boys, without meaning to put them down. A girl raved about a cute boy and the boy called her his girl, not his woman. Just as my married children will never be anything but my children, so the women who lived in my hall will always be "my girls," my daughters-in-affection.

When I wasn't asleep or getting dressed, I left my door open so they'd know they were welcome to come and talk. They would rush in to tell me about an unexpectedly good grade, or a job they'd got, or lesser happenings, or, quite often, very troubling ones.

Listen, I kept telling myself. Don't say anything. They're lectured to all day. When they get out of class, they want someone to listen to them.

The first weeks, I never went upstairs, though I was responsible for the whole building. I didn't want the girls to think I was checking on them. Then we had a flu epidemic— sixty cases in my hall alone. The college doctor and nurses never came to the dormitories. No matter how sick a girl might be, she walked half a mile to the antiquated infirmary on Brattle Street, unless her housemother drove her there. After a couple of students on other campuses had died, the deans realized that this epidemic was serious. They considered turning the gym into an emergency ward but were unable to secure enough nurses. The doctor said there was nothing one could do for flu, anyway. The girls might as well stay in their own rooms. After all, they were adults. They could take care of themselves.

They were adults, all right, but mighty sick ones. And my girls were my girls. So I walked those corridors till I thought I'd drop with fatigue, going from room to room, sticking thermometers into fervish mouths, then going around again to collect and shake the thermometers down.

There was something one could do, even if it wasn't a cure. One could let the patients know that somebody cared enough to come.

Pathetic little notes were shoved under my door late at night by friends of the victims. "Please come to 409. We feel *awful*. Anne and Linny." It had been a hard day but, grabbing my housecoat, I climbed the stairs again because the elevator was apt to get stuck between floors and which maintenance man would come and rescue me in the middle of the night?

From then on, I wasn't afraid to go upstairs. I doubt if the girls even noticed.

The whole five years I was there, I was homesick. My apartment was fine. I had no housekeeping duties. I loved the job. Still, I longed for home. Strangers were living in it, using my things, indifferent to the associations that made them precious to me.

My homesickness helped me to understand the girls—how they could be crazy to get away from home and yet miss it; how they could be hurt because their parents went right on enjoying life, going to the movies, celebrating birthdays, without them.

The first week, a freshman came to me in great distress. She had cut her finger and she held it as if in fear of bleeding to death. All I saw was a tiny scratch. The pain was obviously not in the girl's finger. Gravely applying antiseptic, I asked whether she'd heard from home yet. Her face lit up. Ever since she arrived, she had been asked about her courses, her payment of fees, her gym uniform. No one was interested in what she cared about most—her family. We talked a while. I told her to come back in a day or two and let me see the wound. She never did. I guess she felt better.

It took this flu epidemic to make me realize that that was

how those miracles of healing were performed—by caring. The girls must have cared about me, too, because I was slowly healing. There wasn't time for grief.

I had to learn a whole new language: what it meant to be "clutched," which happened at exam time, and what it meant to be "took," which often happened when girls went to the boys' rooms.

In the Harvard houses there were no old housemothers to keep the girls from going upstairs. A girl could spend all night there. That was 1957. Sex was still a subject that wasn't discussed in polite society. The Pill hadn't yet come in. Abortion was illegal and risky. By Christmas, three of my freshmen had to get married. By midyears, there were more.

I was distressed.

Rules, naively designed to avoid this, had once been on the books. Since they couldn't be enforced, they were abolished. I was glad to see them go. After all, the college wasn't supposed to be a policeman.

I hoped that the administration would now set about helping students to consider their destinies, to make thoughtful choices, instead of just drifting. But when alma mater stopped spanking her children, she washed her hands of them. In those years, her nurturing was purely academic. It wasn't till later that the art of living began to rate as a liberal art.

Some of those teenage marriages were destined to prove more durable than those of couples who married when they were more mature, but at the time I couldn't know this. I needed the companionship of Friends as I struggled to accept a situation that was unacceptable to me.

The Friends Meetinghouse and Center in Longfellow

Park were within walking distance of the Radcliffe Quad. Every Sunday when I went to meeting I thought about my girls and how I could help them. But I saw no way. Trying to exemplify the ideals I stood for was all I could do.

Friends Meeting at Cambridge was much larger than New Haven Meeting. It included many seasoned Friends whose vocal ministry was more moving than any I had ever heard. They knew the Bible and referred to Quaker history, quoting beautiful seventeenth-century passages.

Listening to them, I felt like one who has lived inland all her life, when she first catches sight of the ocean.

It was such a large meeting that it employed an executive secretary, George Selleck, for whom I had the highest regard. Florence, his wife, made everyone feel welcome. I had known them a long time. They enjoyed coming to my concerts.

I suppose musicians perform for the same reason I write—to communicate their vision and perception of life. Much as I longed in my adolescence to do that with music, too, I never became proficient enough. Suddenly, organizing concerts became my instrument. I couldn't make beautiful music myself but I could provide it for my girls and their friends.

Bruce Simonds played at Holmes with a quartet made up of Boston Symphony men. They proved so popular that I asked them back year after year. When Bruce and Rosalind came and played two pianos, the audience went wild over them. The Stradivarius Quartet was so greatly appreciated that it was invited to play every season. Helen Boatright came from New Haven to sing and, one memorable evening, Ralph Kirkpatrick gave a clavichord recital. Doriot Anthony

Dwyer played the flute for us and Alario Diaz the guitar. Almost before I announced that the tickets were available, they were snapped up.

But, I said to myself at the end of the first season, a concert series doesn't make a music center.

I went to the vice president of the college and asked for permission to use part of the fund for other activities. She told me to do what I wished, so long as it was in the field of music and made the girls happy.

Mildred Freiberg, who had been a pupil of Bruce's when she studied at Yale, held a master class for pianists. Wolfe Wolfinsohn, first violin of the Stradivarius Quartet, coached the chamber music players, going from our library, where a trio was rehearsing, to the dining room, where a quartet was playing, to the living room, where there was another little group.

Sunday afternoons, we had sight-reading sessions for anyone at Harvard or Radcliffe who wanted to play or sing in oratorios.

In our huge dining room, the tables and chairs were pushed to one side. Still, we hardly could stuff everyone in. Wallace Woodworth, the much-loved conductor of the Harvard Glee Club, conducted, marveling that I always managed to line up students to sing or play the solo parts. It was easy. Gifted undergraduates like Lanny Young and Charley Forbes and Dick McIntosh were eager to take part and they brought their friends. Guest conductors came from M.I.T. and Boston University.

The college gave each head resident an allowance to be spent on flowers and the sherry that was served before dinner on the nights that professors were invited. The sherry was not to be given to the students, most of whom hadn't attained the legal drinking age.

The whole first year, I resented having to provide the sherry, not because I don't drink it, but because I didn't want my girls to be treated like juveniles. If they weren't allowed to share what was given to their guests, it ought not to be served.

After that, I refused to serve sherry at Holmes and spent the money allotted for it on flowers, which did a lot to enhance the hall. When professors came to dinner, tired after a busy day and looking forward to their glass of sherry, I explained my reason for depriving them. They were, for the most part, quite understanding.

Then Polly Bunting became president. I told her why I wasn't following orders. She sympathized. Eventually, she announced that since the law allowed minors to drink in their own homes and the halls of residence were the students' homes while they were at college, they would be offered sherry when there were guests. From that time on, I served it.

After my first year in Cambridge, I became involved in Quaker work. I was appointed to the executive board of the American Friends Service Committee's New England branch and became a trustee of the Friends schools in Providence, Rhode Island—first Lincoln, then Moses Brown.

One evening, a half dozen of us met and asked ourselves whether we would be justified in opening a Friends elementary school in Cambridge. That was how the Cambridge Friends School began and I became a trustee of that, too.

The job I had taken purely from necessity was turning into an exhilarating experience.

16

Radcliffe head residents were given two days and nights off each month. During the college vacations, they were locked out of their apartments. I had to visit my children and friends, who were extremely good to me. But I longed to be able to go home.

When I stayed with Bruce and Rosalind, I would stand at their dining room window and look over at my house, which I wasn't entitled to enter because I had rented it. And it was that rent, plus what I saved on food and utilities, not my tiny salary, that I was able to put in the bank.

I even looked longingly at the little shed where Nicky had kept chickens during the war. It stood on the lot adjacent to the house. If only it had plumbing! I could, I thought, be happier in that tiny space than I was as a perpetual visitor.

The lot was on the wooded hillside between Bayberry Road and Whitney Avenue. It belonged to me. I fantasized about building a tiny house on the lot, paying for it with the money I had received for the movie rights to *Now That April's There*.

I asked my brother whether he thought I'd be justified in spending the money. He answered that I wouldn't be spending it; I'd just be investing it differently. As things turned out, I invested it far more profitably.

Dreaming about the house was a solace. I wasn't serious. Building a house all by myself with no one to advise me was unthinkable. Nicky, to whom I would have turned, was no longer at M.I.T. He had been given a fellowship at Kings College, Cambridge. So I was only dreaming.

All through my second homeless summer, I dreamed. An architect was out of the question. If I engaged one, there wouldn't be enough money left to pay for building the house.

I began frequenting paint and wallpaper stores to browse through their books of house plans the way some women hang around fabric stores to browse through their books of dress patterns. It was simple—you just chose your dream house, bought the pattern, cut it out, and ran it up.

In a store in Branford I found a plan for a site nestling into a hillside, like my lot. In the picture, the house was beautiful. It had lovely casement windows and looked just right for me. That plan cost ten dollars. I sent to Chicago for it.

I got the name of a Hamden builder. He did remodelling and had never built a house from the ground up, but he was eager for the chance. I liked him and believed he could do it.

When the plan arrived in the mail, I felt I was almost ready to move in. But since I was building the house it seemed as though the interior layout ought to conform more to my needs. An architect I consulted promised to draw up the plans to my specifications, which seemed simple enough to me, since the outside walls and roof weren't to be changed.

It came time for me to go back to college. The architect had done nothing. In a couple of months, the ground would freeze. If I wanted the builder to lay the foundation before spring, he would have to have the blueprints right away. What could I do? Draw them myself? I didn't know the first thing about drafting.

In my little bedroom at Holmes Hall, away from the eyes of my girls, who would certainly have thought I was crazy, I took my pencil and ruler and drew the floor plan on graph paper exactly the way I wanted it to be.

Then I went down to Harvard Square and had blueprints made, which I sent off to the builder. If there was something wrong with my amateurish plan, he never let me know. By the time I went to Hamden for Thanksgiving, there was a promising hole in the ground.

I moved into my very own house in the summer of 1959. I could make a garden! I could have my friends in! They could even spend the night! If I preferred, I could be alone! I could do anything I wished.

Naive as I was about building, I didn't deserve the house I got. No architect could have made it better. Probably none would have been willing to give me the unconventional floor plan. Apart from the little entrance hall and lavatory, downstairs was all one room—living room, dining room, and kitchen. My parents' large Flemish buffets, which had been made for their Paris apartment sixty years earlier, served handsomely as dividers. With windows on four sides, the room had sunshine all day long.

The Steinway just fitted under the open staircase. At Christmastime, I could still have my annual carol party. Sixty or more people could sit around the piano with the children on the floor. Rosalind would play and Betsy would lead the singing, just as they'd always done.

Upstairs, I had a lovely room with a dressing room and two guest rooms as well as two baths. I could squeeze my whole family into my house.

I would still work in my bedroom. That was a habit I'd never willingly give up. But now I had a table to put my typewriter on and lots of bookshelves and a magnificent desk, designed to fit under the big window and made to order for me in Westerly, the gift of Phebe and Thomas.

What did I need all this work space for? Hadn't my writing career ended when I took the job at Radcliffe? I never had a minute there to write, not even to my children.

Again I was mistaken. In due time, three books would be produced in this room: *Mount Joy, A Procession of Friends,* and *I Take Thee, Serenity.*

Seated at my desk, I could look across Lake Whitney to the Davis Street Bridge and East Rock Park. In the spring, I'd look down onto a sea of dogwood blossoms growing wild in the woods.

It was perfect. But when September came, I had to leave. Still, I had a home to come back to any time I was free.

A week before Christmas, my granddaughter Nancy Kirk Newman was born in Washington, D.C. What a Christmas present! As soon as I could shoo the last straggler out of the hall at the beginning of vacation, I checked all the floors and locked up. Then I flew down to meet Nancy. She has given me the greatest happiness by being the person she is, as well as with her music. Now she's on the way to becoming the sixth physician in my family.

In the spring of 1962, I began to have a leading. I was happy working at Radcliffe, but if I stayed till I was sixty-five, I'd be too old ever to write again.

It was hard leaving the girls and the concerts and the lectures I was entitled to audit. It was harder yet settling down in solitude after the five years at college. But I had an idea for a book.

Friends were deeply disturbed by events in Farmville, Virginia, a little town whose school board had closed the public schools to avoid integrating. The white parents opened private academies for their children. The blacks had no education. This worked the greatest hardship on the seniors in high school, who were unable to graduate.

I made contact with some of the Farmville blacks. Then I flew to Richmond and rented a car.

Farmville is so small that any stranger is recognized at once and the authorities were especially on the lookout for white people, like the Quakers, who were outraged by the situation and only came, the authorities believed, to stir up trouble. I only went to observe, though I hoped what I wrote after I left would make more people aware of what was happening.

From the moment I drove into town, I was followed by the police. At every stop sign I brought the car to an exaggeratedly long halt. A traffic violation might be blown up into a much graver charge. The police knew their suspicion was well founded when I parked the car before the home of a black minister, the spokesman for his people.

By arrangement, I met the black visiting nurse there. She took me on her rounds in the county. We passed padlocked school buildings, idle school buses, and went into the most dilapidated shacks I had ever seen. In each of them, ragged children sprawled on the floor in front of the television set. This was all the education they had.

The visiting nurse then took me to her office in the basement of the town hall, next to the jail cells. In front of the bars were the litters on which protesters who had taken part in the "kneel-in" the previous Sunday were carried to jail. They had been praying and singing hymns too fervently in front of a white church during the service.

When I was back in New England, I visited some of the Farmville boys and girls who had been brought north by the American Friends Service Committee so they could finish high school. They had found foster homes with whites who pitied their situation. The relationship of these children and their foster parents was very touching. It called for far more understanding than we in New Haven had been obliged to cultivate when we took the English children into our homes during the war.

One of the girls I visited moved me particularly. She would soon graduate. I imagined the tense and dramatic events—her parting with her foster family in the Springfield, Massachusetts, bus station and being met by her mother and siblings at the bus station in Farmville. She was a very lovable girl. The parting in Springfield must have been a wrench. She returned home not only with a high school diploma, but with a knowledge of the world few Farmville blacks had.

I wanted to witness her homecoming so I joined her in New Haven. She had chosen a seat at the rear of the bus and I took the one next to her. We travelled all night. When we reached Richmond in the morning, I couldn't wait for my coffee. I hoped to take my companion to breakfast but she wouldn't come into the restaurant with me. I tried to explain that it was desegregated now, that she had as much right to go in there as I did. She simply said she wasn't hungry.

When we rolled into Farmville, she pointed out her mother and little brothers. They were standing in front of the waiting room under the sign: Colored. It had been thinly painted over but was still legible. The mother greeted me warmly as we got out. She hastily thanked me for all that had been done for her daughter. Then, in the twinkling of an eye, the whole family vanished. They couldn't risk being caught talking to me.

I felt so moved by the experience that, when I was home again, I started writing immediately. *Love More Sincerely,* I called the piece, quoting, "Carry me back to old Virginny."

Nobody wanted that story.

17

Since this is meant to be simply a literary autobiography, not the story of my life, I wouldn't mention my grandchildren, were they not foremost in the company of those who have contributed to the insight and feeling that I wish my novels to reflect. I was privileged to see a good deal of those children while I was writing the later books. The joyous affirmation in the books can be traced to the happiness and deepened understanding of human nature the grandchildren have given me.

Carol Anne Newman was born in Washington, D.C., in June 1964, completing the family and adding luster to it with her gaiety and enterprise.

That summer, I visited a work camp on the Passamaquoddy Indian Reservation in eastern Maine. It was organized by the American Friends Service Committee. As a member of the New England branch of the committee, I went to observe. The work campers, quartered in a little two-room schoolhouse, were there to assist the Indians in any way they could. They found a lot to do. Conditions on the reservation were deplorable.

When I rolled out my worn sleeping bag in the girls' dormitory—one of the two rooms—I badly crowded my twelve roommates who slept on the floor all summer.

I was writing a novel for teenagers that would have seemed wholly unrelated to this scene, were I not aware by then that my other activities invariably have some unexpected bearing on my writing.

The novel was *Mount Joy,* the story of Maris, who, at the end of her freshman year in college, decides to drop out and make a pilgrimage. She has had a troubling relationship with a boy in her class. It has confused her. All she knows is that she's crazy about the art and architecture of the Middle Ages and she wants to follow the Way of St. James, the old pilgrimage route from Paris to Santiago de Compostela in the north of Spain.

It seemed to me that a pilgrimage eventually leads back to the place from which the pilgrim started. But the person who returns is not quite the same as the one who set out. The returning pilgrim has pursued an aspiration, has had an exhilarating experience, has become aware of new meaning in life.

Maris undertook her pilgrimage without any intimation of this. She simply felt vaguely driven to find out what she was going to do with her life, to understand the nature of the love she was seeking, to discover a religious context in which she belonged. Where all this would lead, she didn't know.

I, however, realized even before I began her story that I must provide Maris with an important place to look back on and perhaps return to, though she can't grasp its significance until she reaches the goal of her pilgrimage three thousand miles away.

When Maris went to say good-by to her grandfather, who lived in Maine, he took her to see the Indians on the reservation. Curious tourists are always driving in there, deploring the conditions they see, then forgetting about them as soon as they drive out. Maris will remember and come back someday to help.

Ralph, one of the work campers, took me from shack to shack, the way Maris's grandfather does in the book. I met many of the Indians, who were appealing, and saw how they lived.

In the little country church, a nun showed me the Indian carvings on either side of the chancel. As I stood before those primitive bas-reliefs, I realized that I was witnessing for Maris the American counterpart of her beloved medieval sculpture.

When she was about to leave, her grandfather gave her a silver pin shaped like a scallop shell, the badge of St. James. Maris fastened it on her beret.

"Au revoir," her grandfather said, hugging her. "Make a good pilgrimage. It's the hardest thing anyone can do."

When I came home from the reservation, I read everything I could find about the medieval pilgrams—their motivation, the art and architecture they created as they travelled through France and northern Spain. I studied the twelfth-century *Pilgrim's Guide,* which described for the people of that time the terrain they would cover and the character of the inhabitants they would encounter on the Way of St. James. It told which regions had the best food, where the water was polluted, what bridges were hideouts for robbers, which ferrymen would throw the pilgrims overboard to obtain their possessions.

It never occurred to me that I would have to make the pilgrimage myself. But as I wrote the opening chapters, the need to go to Santiago became insistent—the need to go alone, as Maris felt obliged to do. I had to know how she felt on the long road. I, too, wished to visit the ancient cathedrals, gaze at the sculpture and the stained-glass windows. Above all, I wanted to see Roncevaux, where Roland died and the *Chanson* turned his defeat to triumph. Travelling in local trains and buses, I could also meditate on life and I could make friends with people who were going my way.

How frightening to leave home for the unknown countryside so far away! Few foreigners penetrated there. But if Maris was going to travel alone, shouldn't I have the courage to do it?

The moment came when I could no longer withstand the compulsion to pin a silver scallop shell on my beret, pack the barest essentials, and sling the bag over my shoulder. I flew to Paris and stayed in the student hostel where Maris and her friend Lonsie would stay, further into the book.

With the help of a Cambridge Friend, who was serving as cultural attaché to the American embassy, I secured permission to attend mass in Chartres Cathedral with the eight thousand university students who were also making a pilgrimage—this one to the shrine of the Virgin Mary—walking the fifty miles from Paris to Chartres on the first weekend in May.

It was thrilling to be there, in this crowd of young people, whose faces showed how deeply they were moved.

Then I went on, travelling by train through the west of France to the Spanish border. Maris and I both had difficulty crossing the Pyrenees by public transportation. I was even more surprised than she was to find myself hitchhiking.

In Spain, women were as troubled about my travelling alone—at my age!—as the ones in the book were about Maris. Pamplona, Puente la Reina—the bridge at which the pilgrims coming from France joined those who came from Italy—Burgos, Leon—Maris and I passed from place to place.

Near Santiago, I met pilgrims, crowds of them, and I saw the gravity of their faces as they prepared to meet St. James.

As soon as I reached town, I went to the cathedral. In the Portico of Glory, St. James is seated high up against the central capitals. It's a glorious statue, much larger than life, yet I felt this might well have been the fisherman who dropped his nets when Jesus called.

But the saint also had a less holy side. Over the centuries, he was used for political propaganda. In Spain's struggle with the Moors he was billed as "The Moorslayer," a bloodthirsty warrior, gloating as his horse trampled upon the bodies of his enemies. And Generalissimo Franco had recruits sent to Santiago to have their banners blessed by the bishop. I saw the recruits kneeling on the pavement in the square before the cathedral, as they swore allegiance to Franco.

Then St. James became gentle again, as pilgrims began filing into the cathedral, with their offerings of gourds or corn and a scallop shell.

When, at last, I climbed Mount Joy, I discovered with great thankfulness that the panorama before me—the mysterious purple mountains encircling the three spires of Santiago Cathedral—wasn't the limit of my vision, the end of my pilgrimage. It was only the beginning.

Upon their arrival in Santiago, the medieval pilgrims were given a scallop shell. I received something equally precious to me—an invitation from Hugh and Shifa Doncaster to visit them in England on my way home.

They lived at The Knapp, a small farm in Worcestershire, and combined market gardening with academic lecturing. Hugh taught at Woodbrooke College, the center for Quaker studies near Birmingham, which attracted scholars from all over the world. Hugh and Shifa—her real name is Cecilia, but nobody calls her that—rigorously maintained the Quaker testimony of simplicity without sacrificing beauty and harmony. These last were visible in the views from the windows of their ancient house, in the books and flowers

that adorned every room, but most of all in their personalities, which reached out in welcome to everyone and
created a serene, comfortable haven for tired friends, both
those who were travel-worn and those who were weary in
spirit.

By the time I had finished the pilgrimage to Santiago
alone, I longed for congenial companionship. This awaited
me at The Knapp.

From England, I went back to Hamden to finish *Mount
Joy.*

But in November, when I was within two chapters of the
end, I almost didn't finish. I was carried away by a dramatic
event in the news. The River Arno had overflowed its banks.
When the water receded, Florence was covered with mud.
Much of her precious art was damaged.

What moved me so deeply that I almost abandoned
Maris were reports that some of the American college
students who had been involved in the campus protests of
the Sixties and had dropped out were converging on Florence, offering to help. Disillusioned, they had left home and
were bumming around Europe. In the States, they were held
in scorn. But when news of the Florentine disaster broke, it
was they, not those who remained in college, who came to
the rescue. Forming a human chain, they pulled art treasures
out of the mud and passed them from hand to hand till the
treasures were brought to safety. They shoveled out cellars,
cleaned statues, spread sheets of rice paper over oil paintings in the churches to absorb the moisture. They worked
long hours.

The city of Florence put them up in army barracks and
gave them one meal a day.

I was impressed by these young people and decided to
write about them. I phoned to the Italian consul to ask

whether I would be allowed to enter Florence if I flew over at once. He said there were no restrictions. I phoned Alitalia Airlines and got a reservation. I made an appointment with my doctor for typhoid shots.

Then I came to my senses. How could I run away and leave *Mount Joy* so close to the end? I had made two trips to Spain for it and invested a lot of time. I had to finish this book first.

I did finish it and sent it off to my literary agent. Then I went to Florence.

It was February by that time. The young Americans who had come to the rescue in Florence's hour of need were exhausted. Most of them had just left. There was no one I could interview, no one I might observe doing heroic work. That was a disappointment.

But I had come to Florence to contribute in some way. So I went to the British consulate, which, I'd been told, was organizing the efforts of both the British and Americans who came to help. I volunteered to do whatever was needed for the next three weeks.

"Oh," the official I spoke to exclaimed, "the National Library is crying for help with the rare books."

I went to the National Library, which is situated right down on the Arno, and had been inundated. At the entrance, there was a high-water mark that came up to my shoulder.

Before the Second World War, the rare books were kept on the top floor of the library and the newspapers in the basement. During the war, a bomb hit the roof of the library. The rare books were hastily carried down to the basement and the newspapers were taken upstairs. Then the flood came, rushing into the basement and drowning millions of precious books.

The British Museum sent a team of experts to repair the

damage. The woman in charge explained the work to me. Pages of the books were discolored by the water. They would look like new after they were put in a special bath and hung up in tobacco sheds around Florence to dry. In order to get them ready for this treatment, the hard covers had to be removed from the books and the linen thread that held the pages together had to be cut.

The museum worker handed me a knife with a narrow blade about a foot long and showed me how to do this, warning me that the knife was very sharp.

I sat down at a table with some young Italians and took a book from the stack that was placed before me. It was a sixteenth-century medical treatise. There were hundreds of other rare books that had to be taken apart.

Just as I was beginning to get a little tired of wielding that knife, I opened another book and could hardly believe my eyes. It was Ferdinand Columbus's account of his father's voyages, published in Venice in 1571—almost four hundred years earlier! I held it between my hands, caressing it, unable to bring myself to slash the cover, although I knew that would be replaced, once the pages were cleaned. I can still feel the reluctance with which I went to work.

On my way home, I stopped in New York to find out how *Mount Joy* was faring.

"Daisy!" my agent exclaimed, when I walked into her office. "The editor I sent *Mount Joy* to can't wait to meet you. She loves the book. What's more, the Junior Literary Guild has selected it."

I was once again an author!

We celebrated by going out to lunch. I was concentrating on the chocolate mousse when the agent turned to me and asked, "How would you like to write a Quaker history?"

18

A Procession of Friends is one of the few Quaker books that did not originate as a concern of Friends. The editors at Doubleday had the idea that, while various religious groups played a significant part in shaping the history of this country, they have only recorded their story for themselves, not for the general reader. To repair this omission, a number of writers were commissioned to prepare volumes for a series to be known as *Religion in America.*

At the end of 1967, I was commissioned to do the Quaker volume. Although it was a project for which I had great enthusiasm, I certainly was not qualified.

"Why are you asking me?" I cried, when Doubleday's religious editor made the suggestion. "I'm not a historian. I'm just a novelist."

"That's what we want," he declared.

The reasoning baffled me.

"No one can really define Quakerism," I argued. "It isn't a body of doctrine. We have no creed. Quakerism is simply a dream—a vision of what we want ourselves and our nation to become. There isn't any one authorized interpretation. There are actually three or four branches of Friends. All have differing views."

The editor laughed. "We're used to that," he told me. "Do you know how many different kinds of Baptists there are?" He went on to discuss what the book should include, observing, "We don't want any theology."

It was then that I thought maybe I could write that book!

"Moreover," he continued, "we would hope that you weren't simply going to tell about the internal workings of the Society. We also want to know about the conflict at the edges—where Quakers tangled with non-Quakers."

Conflict! Didn't conflict permeate the whole history of Friends, not alone at the edges but within the Society itself? The project began to look more and more intriguing.

I was asked to submit a proposal—just two or three pages, the editor said, an outline of what I intended to put in the book.

An outline! I never make an outline. How can I know what's going to happen? The people I'm writing about determine that, whether they are fictional or real. I might well have been the lady Henry Cadbury liked to quote, who said, "How can I know what I think till I see what I say?"

All I could envisage, as I started to write that proposal, was a procession of Friends, one continuous vigil, spanning more than three centuries, stretching from the Atlantic seaboard to the Pacific Coast. So I simply wrote about those people in the order in which they appeared, starting with Mary Fisher and Ann Austin, amongst the first Quakers, if not the very first, to enter the New World, and finishing with contemporary Friends who were pressing for an end to the Vietnam War.

In its chronological place, I told about the Mission to the Gestapo—the effort of three Philadelphia Friends, Rufus Jones, George Walton, and Robert Yarnall, to plead with Adolf Hitler on behalf of the Jews. Friends had a plan for getting the persecuted people out of the country. Seeing Hitler proved impossible but they were allowed to submit their plan to the Chief of the Secret Police. Armed Nazis ushered them into a waiting room at the Gestapo. While the Friends sat there, they bowed their heads and entered into silent prayer. Later they were told that the room was bugged, no doubt in the hope of trapping them. The Quaker silence had innocently outwitted the German Secret Police!

I crammed many other events into the proposal. It came to twenty pages. I had already written a miniature history. The title I chose was *The Business of Our Lives*. This was taken from John Woolman's assertion:

To turn all the treasures we possess into the channel of universal love becomes the business of our lives.

Later, the title was changed to *A Procession of Friends*.

It took the publishers so long to read my proposal that I began to suspect they were choosing another author.

"There," the editor said, when I was finally asked to come in. He pointed to the account of the Quaker meeting in the Gestapo. "This is where we would like your book to begin, with this dramatic incident. The early history can be worked in later. Do you think you could do that?"

The request jolted me. I had been thinking chronologically. How else is history written? But then I saw that this unusual approach freed me. I could write a strictly factual account in the style I was used to, with flashbacks and little revealing anecdotes, which might never have found their way into a conventional history. Obviously, that was what the editors had in mind when they chose a novelist. If the material were to be organized along those lines, the history of Friends in America might be recalled in a fresh and illuminating manner.

I had never attempted any historical writing, apart from a pageant commemorating the three-hundredth anniversary of the arrival of Friends in New England, which was produced by Ruth Osborne at Yearly Meeting in 1956 and again in 1961, when we celebrated the three-hundredth anniversary of the Yearly Meeting. This was history, faithfully researched, but treated fancifully.

Was I capable of writing a proper history?

Lacking confidence, I rushed down to Haverford and asked Henry Cadbury whether he thought I could do justice to the assignment.

Since he appeared to believe that I might, I was emboldened to ask whether he would be my critic.

I told him I wished to be fair to all branches of Friends. "How can I do this," I blurted out, "when I'm such a silent Friend?"

Henry looked at me with that humorous twinkle I found so endearing. "Thee can only write it the way thee sees it," he said.

I knew then that I'd have to enlarge my vision. The following spring and summer I attended eleven Yearly Meetings.

In Westerly, my friend Phebe had died. Thomas was eighty-eight. He was pleased that I'd been offered the commission to write the history. But when I told him that it would take three years, he said sadly, "I don't expect to live to see it published."

At that, I resolved to send him each chapter as it came from the typist.

When the contract was settled, my new editor wrote to me, expressing his pleasure and signing himself, "Your Personal Slave Driver."

I didn't intend to have him looking over my shoulder while I was working, so I wrote back:

Dear Slave Driver,
If you don't know who won the struggle between the slave drivers and the Quakers, you'll find out.

He left me alone.

But the people whose story I set out to tell pushed me

around. They claimed that if a history of Friends was to have validity, it must demonstrate that human beings can be instruments of God. Rather than a chronicle of events, this book must be a record of the testimonies they made. Obviously, there was nothing for me to do but write down what they told me to say.

Even Rimi, the little Italian puppet in a forest-green tunic and rakish fedora, who travelled back and forth across the ocean creating international friendship, demanded a place in the book. His tiny bell, knotted into the neckerchief, tinkled gaily, but his eyes were sad, for the town of Rimini, where he lived, had been devastated in the Second World War. Children who had lost their parents told Rimi their secret sorrow. He comforted them.

A Swiss agency had sent a wonderful woman to Rimini. She collected the orphans and made a home for them in army barracks erected on the rubble. Some of the barracks became classrooms. In one of these, a teacher formed Rimi's head out of papier-mâché. The head was hollow and there was no body in the tunic, only hands sticking out of the sleeves. A child could push his or her forefinger up into the head, the thumb and middle finger into the sleeves, and Rimi immediately responded with love.

Meanwhile, the American Friends Service Committee had organized the School Affiliation Service, which paired American schools with those in devastated countries. Friends Central School outside of Philadelphia became a partner of the school in Rimini. Crayons and colored paper and children's letters began to arrive. The Italian children had nothing to send in return but Rimi. He made an irresistible emissary, travelling back and forth with gifts and messages, cultivating friendships.

I travelled between the two schools as well, observing the international understanding that Rimi fostered. And I became inspired to write Rimi's story, not for publication, only for the children and teachers in both schools. This became a picture book. My neighbor, Bob Rubenstein, who was a psychiatrist by trade, made the most engaging illustrations, giving Rimi his personality and showing the puppet's tender feelings. Brigitte de Werra, a young Swiss woman who had taught in Rimini, translated the English text into Italian and I put the two languages side by side in the book.

When I was writing *A Procession of Friends,* describing Quaker efforts to foster peace and international understanding, it seemed to me that Rimi belonged in that book, too, even if it was intended for adults.

Recollecting the past in the context of the present, I began to see a pattern emerge. Certain testimonies were repeated throughout Quaker history. The Gestapo in Berlin in 1938 recalled the Lion's Den in Boston, the prison where Friends were tortured, in 1658. Efforts of Little Rock Friends to integrate their schools in 1957 recalled John Woolman's concern for the slaves in 1757. Friends aboard the *Golden Rule* sailed out into the Pacific hoping "with the weight of their whole lives" to stop the nuclear weapons tests just three hundred years after those aboard the *Woodhouse* sailed across the Atlantic, "moved of the Lord to look the bloody laws (of Boston) in the face."

Before the *Golden Rule* set sail, the crew addressed a letter to President Eisenhower. "We are here because stopping preparation for nuclear war is now the principal business of our lives," they wrote. "It is also the principal requirement for the continuation of human life."

Friends are still protesting preparation for nuclear war, not "with the weight of their whole lives," but often at the cost of their freedom.

Sometimes Friends reminded me of Sisyphus in the *Odyssey,* who kept pushing that stone uphill, only to have it roll down as soon as it reached the top. But Friends didn't give up. On the way to Germany in 1938, Rufus Jones, who was seventy-five, wrote in his diary:

We need the note of adventure, of the heroic and costly, not the twittering of birds over a volcano.

19

The Mission to the Gestapo did not change the course of events. It did not prevent the slaughter of six million Jews any more than the Friends who'd been banished from Boston and returned at the cost of their lives succeeded in stopping the persecution. But in both instances, Friends made a clear, courageous testimony. For me, the Quaker witness is more authentic because a Meeting for Worship after the manner of Friends was held in the headquarters of the German Secret Police.

Seventeenth- and eighteenth-century Friends, who recorded the stirring events of their time, set a standard of sonority and vitality in their prose that I couldn't hope to attain. My ability to communicate in contemporary terms wasn't equal to the grandeur of the history. Anything inferior seemed sacrilegious.

After I had written the first few chapters I read them over and thought they sounded dreadful. How could I ever have dreamed that I was capable of writing this history? The only thing to do was break the contract and give the money back.

It seemed wise to consult someone first. So I sent the chapters to Gordon Browne, my trusted critic. After a time, I went down to Cape Cod and asked him whether he didn't think, too, that I should give up the history and start a novel instead.

Gordon tested my commitment. Did I really wish to write this book? Or did I prefer to give it up in favor of a novel?

I told him how fervently I wished to write the history; I just didn't feel I was doing it well.

Gordon listened quietly. Then he said, "I hope it won't hurt your feelings, but I think this book will be read after your novels are forgotten."

However that may be, I went home and plugged away.

As each of the forty-four chapters was completed, I sent it to Thomas. He would write or telephone his comments. There were times when I thought I would collapse under the weight of those footnotes and the whole responsibility. His encouragement sustained me.

In Richmond, Indiana, Errol Elliott was reading the proof of his history, *Quakers on the American Frontier.* I didn't know him, but I wanted to learn about pastoral Friends. So I flew out to see him and gained a great deal of insight.

On the Island of Nantucket, George Selleck was also writing history—the book that was to become *Quakers in Boston.* In the summer, I sailed over from Woods Hole and we discussed each others' work.

In March of 1968, George wrote to me:

As you doubtless observed in what I wrote earlier, I was having trouble defining what history is. My first impulse was to say that a historian simply presents the facts and lets them speak for themselves. . . . But then I found that the facts do not speak for themselves. One has to give them a voice. History, I found, is discovering the pattern that gives the facts significance, and the discovery of that pattern involves an act of imagination, of deliberately venturing beyond anything the facts may present. For a while then I had difficulty seeing the difference between history and fiction. But then I saw that the pattern of history must correspond, if it is true, as exactly as possible to the pattern of the events recorded . . . history is not just facts. It is the discovery of those ideas, purposes, and their interplay that give meaning to events. So now I feel much more akin to the novelist than I did formerly.

George's theory helped me to understand why the publishers had chosen a novelist to write history. Was I capable of "discovering the pattern that gives the facts significance"?

How could I fail, with the immediacy of world events in those years? I wasn't only writing history. I was witnessing it in the making. Just after the book was begun, during the Tet offensive of 1968, Marjorie Nelson, a young Quaker doctor from Indiana, who was treating civilian war casualties—many of them children—in the Friends Rehabilitation Center in Quang Ngai, was captured by the Viet Cong. Fifty-two days later, she was released and told to leave the country.

Marge stayed home for a short time. Then she went back to Vietnam to complete her two-year term of service. To me, this seemed as courageous an act as Mary Dyer's returning to Boston after she'd been warned that, if she did, she'd be hanged.

I was beginning to appreciate my good fortune in being appointed to spend three years in the company of Friends who, in their time, testified to what they believed. They weren't all heroes, but at some point in their lives they were heroic. It got to be a love affair. I couldn't wait to start work each morning. I began getting up earlier and earlier.

Some of the research was done at Haverford College and Friends House, London, but most of it in the Yale Library, which turned out to have a good Quaker collection. Climbing up and down the narrow marble stairs in the stacks, I got very tired. It was eerie, too. There was never another soul in the wing where they kept the Quaker books. I began to have a fantasy about curling up on one of the empty shelves and going to sleep.

In June, Tom Bodine and I attended the Friends General Conference at Cape May, New Jersey.

A Philadelphia Friend took Tom aside and asked, "What in the world does Daisy Newman think she's doing, writing a history of Friends?"

I asked myself the same question every time I looked over my chapters. Henry Cadbury read them during the conference. That cheered me.

Tom and I had the good fortune to share a table in the hotel dining room with Henry and Lydia. Our meals were hilarious. We laughed so much that the other guests kept trying to overhear our conversation. It wasn't difficult. The Cadburys were both very deaf.

That Sunday, while we were sitting on the sunny jetty, worshipping, other Friends were sitting in the Washington, D.C., jail, testifying to their solidarity with the Poor People, whose "Resurrection City, U.S.A."—the plywood shacks in which they camped while they pleaded with Congress for more food—had been demolished by the police. The Poor People and their sympathizers marched to the Capitol and were arrested. They did not succeed in obtaining more food.

In August, Friends Meeting at Cambridge gave sanctuary to Eric, an AWOL soldier, who wished to be classified as a conscientious objector. One Sunday morning after meeting, he was introduced to Friends. Then he held a news conference in the Center, stating his reasons for having run away from the army when he was about to be shipped to Vietnam.

In the meetinghouse, Friends did not close meeting as usual that morning. They continued to worship in support of Eric until he should be arrested. They expected this to take place immediately. But the police did not arrive.

Over in the Center, Friends cooked lunch for Eric and his friends.

Word quickly got around Harvard Square. In no time, the meetinghouse lawn swarmed with types very different from

those usually seen there on First Day. Bare feet, mini-
miniskirts, which were still a shock, guitars—Longfellow
Park had never looked like this.

Most of those who suddenly came didn't know what a
Quaker was. They came because this was where the action
was and they opposed the draft and the war. They claimed,
as Friends do, that the State does not have authority over
their consciences, but few of them would have relegated
that authority, as Friends do, to God.

Toward night, a cot was put up for Eric in the meetinghouse basement where, by day, used clothing is mended and
sent to the needy overseas.

The Friends who had kept the meeting going all day
went home. Others came to take their places. The Meeting
for Worship continued all night.

The next day, people began arriving from all over Boston
and the suburbs. They had heard the news on the radio or
TV. They wanted to add their weight to the witness. Protes-
tant ministers, rabbis, nuns in their new, short habits, and
priests filled the meetinghouse benches. Others came who
weren't interested in religion but were opposed to the war.

To their surprise, they all felt easy here. There were no
symbols to rebel against, no words to repeat that they might
not believe. There was only the healing silence, interrupted
from time to time by people who felt deeply moved—
ordinary, searching people, like themselves—telling simply
what lay on their hearts. The passionate longing for peace
that hung over the countryside had found a focus. The ache
all these people brought with them, remembering someone
in Vietnam or the doom that threatened their children,
received a promise of surcease.

Someone rose, moved to speak. "Wherefore," he quoted,
"seeing we also are compassed about with so great a cloud
of witnesses, let us lay aside every weight. . . ."

Throughout the bright afternoon, young people who had never been in the meetinghouse entered and sat down near Eric, betraying in the way they carried themselves that this short time together was precious.

Then it was dark again. The Friends who came to hold meeting through the night brought their toothbrushes so they could go straight to work in the morning, just as those who went to meeting in the seventeenth century, when Quaker worship was unlawful, brought their nightcaps with them because they knew that by bedtime they'd be in jail.

Then it was morning. Still, the police didn't come. In the Friends Center, volunteers prepared meal after meal.

Under the maple on the lawn, a little group sat, singing and playing guitars. The young Friends taught their visitors a Quaker song:

> Stand in the light, wherever you may be!
> Stand in the light, wherever you may be! In your old leather
> breeches and shaggy, shaggy locks
> You're walking in the glory of the light, George Fox.

"Stand in the light," the women in the kitchen of the Friends Center echoed, while they stirred spaghetti and meatballs for the ever-growing number of Eric's hungry friends. "Stand in the light, wherever you may be!"

On the tenth morning, a Radcliffe girl came running across the lawn. "The Russians have invaded Czechoslovakia!" she shouted.

The enormity of this new assault on freedom was beyond anyone's power to grasp in the summer sunshine. In Czechoslovakia this morning, Friends wouldn't be allowed to sit quietly, upholding a young man's right to refuse what the government decreed. They'd simply be mowed down by tanks.

On the eighteenth day, two officers arrived with a

warrant for Eric's arrest. A Friend greeted them in the driveway and explained that a Meeting for Worship was in progress. Would the officers come into the meetinghouse and join in the silence until the meeting was brought to a close?

The officers came in quietly and listened, as Friends spoke under the leading of the Spirit. When hands were clasped all around, the officers served the warrant and took Eric away.

This was history in the making. It became the subject of the chapter in *A Procession of Friends* entitled "Quaker Hospitality."

The Cottonwood Foundation gave the Friends World Committee for Consultation a grant that enabled me to attend Yearly Meetings in Iowa, Pennsylvania, North Carolina, Indiana, Ohio, and California.

On the Sunday of Philadelphia Yearly Meeting in 1970—Easter Sunday—Marjorie Nelson was married to Robert Perisho, a graduate student at Yale. The most important guests at the wedding were some wounded Vietnamese children in wheelchairs, whom Marge had treated when she was working in Quang Ngai. They had been sent to Philadelphia for surgery. The occasion struck me as an eminently significant one in the annals of Friends and so this wedding dominated the last chapter. When, only a few years later, Bob Perisho died, it seemed even more fitting that this beautiful wedding had been recorded.

Five xeroxed sets of the manuscript began circulating among some twenty-five readers, for I had come to think of this not as my book but as a corporate concern. I tried out a few chapters on a Roman Catholic nun. Henry Cadbury read the manuscript at four different stages. I took it to England twice, where Elfrida Vipont Foulds, the Quaker historian, read it and Hugh Doncaster read it aloud to Shifa and me in their garden during apple blossom time.

There were many others on whose judgment I relied. In the Foreword I tried to convey how impossible it would be to name them all.

In the Meeting for Worship after the manner of Friends, it sometimes befalls that a person who feels moved to break the silence and share a fresh insight unknowingly expresses the thoughts of those listening. The speaker is not speaking *to* the Meeting; the gathered Meeting is speaking *through* one member.

So may the company of people with whom, over the years, the writer has worshipped and worked out concerns speak through this book. Like "many candles, lighted and put in one place," they have made the light "more to shine forth." They have added their scholarly achievements, their loving concern, and that characteristic humor with which Friends make little of the weightiest assignments. To name them would require another volume. . . .

The writer has no way of expressing her gratitude to them. . . . Like William Penn she can only exclaim, "O that they that read me could but feel me!"

20

Shortly after *A Procession of Friends* went to press, I had an invitation from the editor of *Mount Joy.* "Now you're free," she wrote. "Wouldn't you like to write the novel you once talked about—nineteen-year-olds getting married?"

I thought I would. Ever since I was a housemother, I've had a concern for girls as they make the perilous journey from adolescence into adulthood, especially those who enter into marriage before they've had time to grow up.

Young couples with no religious ties, who abhorred the pomp often associated with church weddings, were asking to be married after the manner of Friends. Because this is an extremely simple ceremony, performed without a clergyman or other authoritarian figure, the young people assumed mistakenly that a Quaker wedding makes a minimum of demands. They were often surprised to discover the depth of commitment that such a marriage signifies to the strangers under whose care it is accomplished and the responsibility Friends feel for the future welfare of the couple.

Teenagers who might have begun a relationship with merely sexual love find that they have a distance to travel before arriving at the commitment implied in a Quaker marriage.

I longed to write about becoming—becoming a young adult, competent, sensitive, assured, part of a caring community; about becoming a wife or husband; about becoming joyful.

It seemed to me that Friends of my generation were better able to help these youngsters than their parents were, not by dictating standards or by leaving the youngsters value systems to be formed by their peers, but by providing a serene setting, a quietude in which they might learn from their Inward Teacher, as Friends call the Light that shines in each of us. Older Friends are in the position to be fellow pilgrims, accompanying the youngsters in their search, supporting them with an impersonal love.

What is needed, I thought, as I reflected on the young people I was being invited to write about, is not precept but identification with an ideal. Fiction can furnish that.

I sensed great hunger among the young for a different kind of inspiration than they were getting in much of their reading. If some of John Woolman's writings were quoted in a novel, they would, I felt, have a strong appeal.

There is a principle which is pure, placed in the human mind, which in different places and ages hath had different names. It is, however, pure and proceeds from God. It is deep and inward, confined to no forms of religion, nor excluded from any, where the heart stands in perfect sincerity . . .

Which seeker, young or old, could resist those words? Or:

Wealth is attended with power, by which bargains and proceedings contrary to universal righteousness are supported; and here oppression, carried on with worldly policy and order, clothes itself with the name of justice and becomes like a seed of discord in the soul.

Following on their concerns of the Sixties, young readers would find Woolman's sentiments confirming.

I assumed that the editor had in mind an adult novel that would also be appropriate for "young adults." The invitation excited me. It was as if the characters were already somewhere in my mind, just waiting to be called into existence. What a temptation!

But I had begun research for a biography and it seemed wrong simply to drop that.

The childhood of the Mozarts had always intrigued me. Early in my career, I had written an unsuccessful juvenile about little Wolfgang. Now it was Nannerl whose life story I wished to portray. What was it like for her, the highly gifted musician, when her little brother outshone her? How could she have helped being jealous? What became of her later? The Mozart biographies scarcely mention Nannerl after she stopped being a prodigy. And yet, I discovered, as I began looking into it, she outlived the genius by nearly forty years.

Unlike her brother, Nannerl never revolted against Leopold, their domineering father, and she couldn't forgive Wolfgang for marrying against the father's wishes. She was so obedient that she gave up the man she loved because he didn't have brilliant enough prospects to suit the grasping Leopold. Instead, Nannerl married a disagreeable widower who not only had means but—most coveted of all—a title, even if only a petty one. He also had five unruly children. Living deep in the country, Nannerl was out of touch with the musical life of Salzburg. While her brother was at the height of his success, she was relegated to domesticity.

Nannerl impressed me as a dramatic subject for a biography. I had no difficulty reading the German and I had already learned the little that seemed to be known about her. Why was I putting off writing?

What held me back was a growing awareness that there was no documentation for the affairs of daily life that make a biography interesting and I had scruples about inventing them. Leopold's letters to Nannerl are full of details concerning his household. She evidently treasured those letters. They still exist. But I knew of none that she had written to her father.

Perhaps if I were to go to Salzburg, I'd find the documented material I needed. There must be unpublished manuscripts in the Mozarteum. But I had no immediate plans for going to Europe and I wasn't sure that this biography was promising enough to warrant the expense.

Something else troubled me: the events following the birth of Nannerl's first child were bizarre, indeed suspicious. That would make a juicy novel—the kind I didn't care to write. I wasn't willing to hint at a scandal, especially since it could not be substantiated. I found myself obliged to acknowledge that this was a subject for a biographical novel.

I'm not critical of authors who write biographical novels, if they don't pretend that what they make up actually happened. But it's a type of book I wouldn't enjoy writing.

The novel about youngsters getting married offered a way out. Still, I hesitated. I had invested a great deal of time researching the Mozart material and I really was deeply sympathetic with Nannerl.

Jimmy, my grandson, was fourteen. He was having trouble in school with French. All he cared about was skiing. When *A Procession of Friends* went to press, I told him to work harder at his French. I was about to receive the advance that was due on delivery of the manuscript and I could take him to Switzerland during his spring vacation. The snow would be at its best then. If he were able to converse with people, he would have a much better time.

Jimmy's marks improved significantly.

By then, I had decided that I must go to Salzburg. I made definite plans to do that after leaving Switzerland.

We were seen off from Boston by somewhat apprehensive parents. But we managed very well indeed.

When we reached Geneva and rode in from the airport, I was sorry that Jimmy's first impression of Switzerland should be of rather drab houses set in an unspectacular landscape. The boy must be disappointed.

Nothing of the kind! He was ecstatic. "All those foreign cars!" he exclaimed. "I never saw so many."

From the train that skirted the Lake of Geneva, he got his first view of the mountains and he appreciated them, too, though perhaps less. But the little cog railway that makes the ascent from Bex to Villars was a huge success.

We had a glorious week. Jimmy joined a ski class and spent most of the day on the mountainside. In the evening, he heard French being spoken on the pension's television set. Even the commercials were instructive.

For me, coming to Villars was like coming home, except that the place had become a busy winter sports resort, very different from the quiet village that Dick and Ellen and I knew forty years earlier.

Coming back to those mountains was of itself worth the journey. They had enlarged my vision when I spent a year in their sight, learning to read their moods, watching them emerge from the clouds as the weather cleared. Twenty-three years later, in my darkest moment, they assured me that the Inward Light is ever present, even when it is thickly veiled, and I came to see how minuscule were my life and its disappointments, measured against the majesty of the Dents du Midi.

At the end of our week in Villars, Jimmy and I went to Lausanne to visit my young friends, Brigitte and Dominique. Then we went to Geneva, where we parted, Jimmy to fly back to Boston and I to go on to Salzburg, full of hope.

And Salzburg itself didn't disappoint me. The town had all the charm I expected to find. I visited the birthplace of the Mozart children and the palace where they performed. I located the house facing the Universitätsplatz where Nannerl lived when she moved back to Salzburg after the death of her husband. I went to the cemetery, where there is a portrait, made in her old age.

I listened raptly to the timbre of the bells that struck against each other every hour. For days, I wandered through the old town, taking everything in. It was beautiful. And yet, I was to come away empty-handed.

Although Walter Grossmann, the librarian of the University of Massachusetts, had given me a letter of introduction to the librarian of the Mozarteum, who was extremely courteous in the Austrian manner, I was not shown any documents that weren't already in print. I may have been mistaken, but I couldn't help feeling that there must be something the authorities wished to conceal.

From Salzburg I flew to England.

The youth hostel in Holland Park had long been my London club. It was probably the quietest guest house in central London, located as it was in the middle of a large, very beautiful park. One couldn't drive up in a taxi. One had to walk from the Bayswater Road or Kensington, carrying knapsack and sleeping bag. I loved it.

Unlike most youth hostels, George V Hostel served breakfast and supper. I met people there from all over the world. They were friendly, not standoffish, as one has to be in a hotel. And it was cheap. The warden came to know me. She always managed to give me a bed, even on short notice. I was probably the oldest youth in the hostel.

After a few days in London, I visited the Doncasters again. As the train pulled into the Worcester station, I caught sight of Hugh standing on the platform, waiting for me. When we were in his car he looked at me before turning on the ignition. "How is thee?" he asked.

"Fine," I answered, or something equally noncommittal.

But Hugh persisted. He must have seen in my face that I was struggling with a big decision. "How is thee in thyself, Daisy?"

I said nothing then.

When we reached The Knapp, there was Shifa, waiting to embrace me.

During tea, I told them that I was trying to decide which of two books I would write first. Fresh from Salzburg, I described the charm that the Mozart scene had for me and also my disappointment in not having learned more there. Then I confided my deep concern for young people and the opportunity I had to write about them. I spoke, too, of the appeal I believed the writings of John Woolman would have for the young.

When I was leaving, as Hugh drove me to the station, he said, "I don't want to influence you but—anyone could write that biography. Only you have those troubled young people in mind who discover Friends. What greater service could you render?"

I had never thought of a novel as service. Even now, when I've received such a quantity of letters from unknown readers all over the country, who tell me how the faith and hope in my books have spoken to them, often at a time of deep personal trouble, I still think a novel is simply a work of art. If it serves someone in need, that's just a happy accident.

What Hugh said did influence me. I thought about it all the way home. But when I got there, I was still undecided.

A Procession of Friends was just out and I took the first copy to Thomas. He had had his ninety-second birthday. He couldn't have read the book anymore, but he knew what was in it and he looked very happy, just holding it in his hands.

Six weeks later, he died.

We had been friends for twenty-six years. In him, I had

seen the embodiment of that spirit that had drawn me, long before I knew him, to Quakerism. And, as with Henry Cadbury, Moses Bailey, and many other Friends, this spirit was leavened with endearing humor.

I thought, if I have the skill to communicate what it meant to be in the presence of someone who was earnestly trying to live in the presence of God, his spirit will go right on living, not just for those who were privileged to know him but for my readers, too.

That's when I decided to write the book that became *I Take Thee, Serenity*. The character of Oliver Otis was already established.

21

Oliver would be an old Quaker farmer. A Harvard graduate, son of a professor, he has spent his life caring for Firbank, his Grandmother Serenity's farm near the shore in southern Rhode Island.

During the First World War, he was a conscientious objector. After the war, he went to France to help with the reconstruction of bombed-out villages. There he met Daphne, an English Quaker who was assisting in the repatriation of prisoners of war. Daphne marries Oliver and goes to the States with him, where she makes a name for herself as a painter.

At the time of the Vietnam War, Oliver becomes so outraged by his country's practice of defoliating trees that he has to do something. He thinks that if he can only find a formula for restoring the trees, once hostilities cease Vietnam can be made capable of sustaining life again.

He goes to the university and asks the foresters for advice.

When I got to this point, I realized that I would have to start by doing the same thing. So I went to the Connecticut Agricultural Experiment Station and consulted a soil expert.

I considered this idea of Oliver's a quixotic dream, not an objective that could be realized. As I explained Oliver's actions, I said, "I know he can't succeed, but he's the idealistic type. He has to try, even if he's bound to fail."

The expert surprised me by saying, "He needn't fail. Here at home, where herbicides have been applied in lethal doses as weed killers, farmers have used deactivated charcoal to restore the soil."

I was overjoyed. Oliver needn't fail! But he will have to work very hard to find the formula.

Early in the book, he will succeed in helping Serenity.

Named for her Quaker great-grandmother, nineteen-year-old Serenity is anything but serene. In love with Peter and confused by her worldly parents, she bravely sets out for a strange place called Firbank, in search of her father's cousin Oliver, whom she doesn't know.

Her parents, eager to put a good face on what they suspect is a bad situation, plan an elaborate church wedding, although they have no religious ties. But Serenity thinks that if her parents insist on this marriage, which she and Peter don't feel ready for, they would prefer the simplicity of a wedding conducted after the manner of Friends. Actually, Serenity doesn't know what that's like.

It is in the hope of discovering this and arranging for the wedding that, without telling her father, Serenity goes to see Oliver.

I could hear them talking when they met. It was as if they were people I'd been associated with all my life. And, in a sense, they were—paper people who communicated my own adolescent yearning for a wise and idealistic friend. Now, Oliver and Serenity came tumbling onto the pages faster than I could type.

Firbank had been with me a long time, too, though it's not to be found on the map of Rhode Island, any more than the township of Kendal. It's only on the chart of my inner landscape. Firbank will always be a refuge when we fear that our world will be blown to bits and we are powerless to avoid this destiny.

Just as Oliver's faith and dogged persistence prove that the evil of defoliation can be reversed, so, if we believe God means our planet, with its beauty and inherent goodness, to survive—not just for us but for all people—and we work with Oliver's dedication to overcome the nuclear threat, we may yet succeed.

When Serenity's plane comes down in Rhode Island, she loses her nerve and decides to go right back to college. But Oliver is at the airport, waiting for her. He recognizes her by her red curls, the "Otis hair," and takes her to Firbank. This is Serenity's first glimpse of it:

> Oliver stopped the truck before a long, white farmhouse with huge maples at each corner and wisteria hanging in fringes from the roof of a stately, semicircular porch. A lawn separated the house from the driveway. . . . The house needed paint, but, touched by the setting sun, it had a misty, pink radiance, its outline blurring into the atmosphere, so that it was one with the earth, the trees, and the sky that framed it.
>
> That's what I've been missing all along, Rennie said to herself with surprise—beauty! That's the emptiness I feel sometimes, even though Peter and I have the best of both worlds.

By "the best of both worlds," Serenity means what she thinks of as the Garden of Eden, though it's only Peter's drab dormitory room. Their love makes it sunny, a place of completeness, where, she believes, nobody gets hurt. The other world, the one outside, never touches their secret one.

Suddenly she discovers that a great many people are hurt. The outside world butts in, demanding decisions, commit- ment, celebration. It threatens to saddle Serenity and Peter with household linens, place settings, appliances.

In a garden, Serenity thinks, who needs these?

Serenity and Peter and Oliver were familiar to me. But Daphne, Oliver's wife—I didn't know her. She was, I thought, one of those characters in a novel who are created by an author to conform to the exigencies of the plot. Daphne posed a problem because three-way conversation on an intimate level is hard to handle and it was only Oliver, I assumed, who would help Serenity out of her confusion.

Suppose Daphne had suffered a stroke, which robbed her of the power of speech—wouldn't that be a solution? The dialogue would be simplified. After all, Daphne was only a minor character. She didn't need to speak. Yes, Daphne would have aphasia. That would make everything easier.

But how could I describe her? I'd never seen a stroke patient who was afflicted that way. In fact, I knew little about the illness, even though my father died of it. The stroke didn't affect his speech. As often happened fifty years ago, pneumonia carried him off in a few days.

I asked John, my neurologist friend, to tell me what Daphne looked like. He described her paralyzed arm and her lopsided face, the difficulty she had in walking. He made me feel how agonizing it would be to witness her trying to speak. So I was able to proceed. Daphne wouldn't get in my way. She'd just be there.

How imperceptive I was! As soon as Serenity walked in and Daphne, smiling with one side of her face, reached out her left hand, as soon as their eyes met, a relationship of first importance to the plot began. Far from being a minor character, Daphne turned out to be very important. I couldn't direct her. She very nearly ran away with the book. Even after her death, which I hadn't anticipated—she just died, as people do—Daphne continued to exert an influence on those who had known her.

To my surprise, Daphne and Serenity ministered to each other. Daphne reached out in accepting love to the troubled young girl who became devoted to her. Serenity, in turn, inspired Daphne to overcome her handicap and paint Serenity's portrait, the finest of Daphne's career.

"It's much more than the likeness of an individual," Oliver tells Serenity, speaking of the portrait. "It's the dawn of that day we hope thy whole generation will wake to."

So both Daphne and Oliver rescue Serenity from her adolescent confusion. Successful as they are, however, with another couple's daughter, they have failed to communicate their deep caring to their own. Heather, who has adolescent children herself, still clings to the fiction that her parents love each other more than they love her. Nothing could be further from the truth. It's Serenity who helps Heather to realize this.

Serenity and Peter began coming to meeting with me. I'd just be centering down when I'd glance up and there they would be, on the back bench among the latecomers. How did they get there? Oughtn't I to have left my work at home? I felt guilty. But I couldn't stop thinking about their problems and when meeting closed, a solution had come to me.

Then I began to see that paper people have to cultivate the spirit, just like the rest of us. It was fitting that Serenity and Peter come to meeting. Of course! They needed as much as anyone to enter into the presence of God, they who were trying so hard to find their way.

After that, I felt comfortable about their coming. It would have diminished the book to have left them at home. But I did encourage them to get up a little earlier on First Days, so they could sit with me and we could wait for insight together.

Before starting to write, I had to learn about the terrain I wished to describe. Young Tom Perry and Katherine, his wife, walked over it with me, pointing out the birds and the vegetation and the little creatures on the edge of the pond.

Next, I went down to Haverford to see Henry Cadbury. Ever since I began trying to communicate the Quaker way of life in fiction as well as history, I had sought his approval for what I wrote. It wasn't alone his stature as a scholar and his charm as a storyteller that set a standard for me. It was the grace he brought to his work and to his relations with people.

Would he see me through this book, I asked, criticizing it as he had so carefully and generously criticized the others?

For the first time in the three decades that he had been interested in what I was trying to do, he hesitated. "How long will it take?"

"Two years."

"I don't know," he murmured. "I don't want to live to be too old."

He was eighty-eight, but still so full of enthusiasm and fun that I left reassured.

I Take Thee, Serenity was begun in Woods Hole, where I was spending the summer with Nicky and his family.

It was ten years since I left Radcliffe, ten years of germination before what I learned there was transformed into paper people who would touch the hearts of readers as the Holmes Hall girls had touched mine.

22

A few chapters of *I Take Thee, Serenity* were completed when I read in the London *Friend* that Woodbrooke College was organizing a "Woolman Walk" to commemorate John Woolman's walk from London to York in 1772.

He had come to England from New Jersey, sailing steerage because he chose to share the sailors' accommodation. After attending London Yearly Meeting, he set out for York on foot, refusing to travel by stagecoach. He had heard that the excessive speed at which the post horses were driven blinded, even killed them and that the little postboys, who were obliged to ride outside in all weathers, sometimes froze to death.

As Woolman walked, he thought about the oppressed and the poor, observing the low wages that were being paid for a day's work and the high price of food. He noted the pollution of streams and fields, where dyers emptied their vats, and was repelled by "the scent arising from filth which more or less infects the air of all settled towns." On August twenty-third, he reached Preston Patrick, went on to Kendal in what was formerly Westmorland, and turned eastward into beautiful Wensleydale.

Woolman reached York on September twenty-first, entering the town by Bootham Bar. Smallpox had overtaken him on the way. Two weeks later, he died at Almery Garth, York.

A Woolman Walk! I had to go!

It's two hundred miles, my reason told me. You can't walk that far. Besides, the expense of the flight—

So I gave up the idea. But I confided to my children how much I wished I might go.

A few weeks later, Woodbrooke had another notice in the *Friend.* No one, it seemed, could take the time to walk two hundred miles. Therefore the distance was being cut in half.

Even a hundred miles were beyond me. Could I rent a car? Would the Woodbrooke Friends want an elderly American woman in their party, one who could only walk on wheels? I didn't dare write to them for fear of putting them in an embarrassing position. It would be difficult for them to write back, "Dear Friend, We'd ever so much rather thee stayed in America."

So I wrote to Hugh. The next time he lectured at Woodbrooke, would he feel out his colleagues who had announced the walk?

I don't think he did. He simply wrote back:

Come! We'll lend you our car. It's ramshackle, but it usually goes.

Timidly, I wrote to Woodbrooke and got a reply by return mail. I was welcome to join the walkers. I could ride in the car that would be taking the provisions and the bedrolls. However, the walkers would occasionally be sleeping in meetinghouses. Wouldn't that be out of the question for me? Perhaps local Friends would offer to put me up.

I wrote back that I'd want to sleep wherever the walkers did. I'd be very comfortable on a meetinghouse bench.

When I asked Nicky and Kathy what they thought about my making the trip at my advanced age—sixty-eight—they said nothing. But the next morning, when I went into the kitchen for breakfast, there was a big box on my chair. I couldn't imagine what was in it.

Hopping up and down with excitement, Jimmy and Nancy and Carol stood beside me, watching as I opened the box.

A new sleeping bag, much finer than my old, flimsy one! A lovely warm sleeping bag for rolling out on English meetinghouse benches!

Then Ellen offered to contribute to the expense of the flight.

This was my family's way of signifying that they didn't consider me too old for adventure.

Next, Friends in Kendal, England, wrote and invited me to speak about Woolman in their meetinghouse on the Sunday afternoon when the walkers would be having tea there and my dear friend Elfrida wrote that I must stay at her house in Yealand Conyers, when the walkers slept at nearby Preston Patrick.

Henry Cadbury published *John Woolman in England* in 1971. He had spent years piecing together facts culled from various sources, tracing Woolman's journey from London to York. In reply to my letter about my plans, he wrote, "I envy thee the chance to make the pilgrimage." He was no longer able to go to England and pursue his research. But, through his book, he became my constant guide.

Two hundred years after Woolman passed through Westmorland and Yorkshire, ten or so walkers gathered at Preston Patrick Meetinghouse.

From the first hearty meal together, prepared by local Friends, the walkers, who hadn't known each other before, felt knit into a community. They spent the night in the hostel at Preston Patrick. I was fortunate enough to be staying with Elfrida.

The next day, at Brigflatts, we celebrated the eighteenth birthday of Andrew, the youngest walker. He found it espe-

cially congenial to walk beside the retired schoolmaster.
And the youngest woman inserted a poem in our log that
spoke for all of us. Gazing at the countryside between the
River Lune and Morecambe Bay, with its timeless houses and
dry-stone walls, remembering George Fox, when he "sounded the day of the Lord" here after coming down from Pendle
Hill more than three centuries earlier, she wrote:

> Another time, the same place,
> people lived, people worked,
> sharing the great experience of their lives.
> We retrace their footsteps,
> trying to discover or maybe re-discover
> the strength they drew from God.

Each evening, local Friends treated us to high tea and
pressed us to explain our reasons for undertaking the walk.
We found that in worshipping with them and speaking about
Woolman, about whom many British Friends knew little, our
own understanding deepened. The indescribable beauty of
the dales, sparkling in crisp weather, and the closeness we
felt with each other as we travelled together, heightened our
perception. We found we were making a pilgrimage—not to
places sanctified by Woolman but to our own inner landscape, our own Inner Light.

I became quite fond of sleeping on meetinghouse
benches, particularly those that had cushions. The walkers
preferred the floor. They seemed pleased by my wish to
share their accommodation. Every morning, one of the men
brought us each a cup of tea, which gave us the strength to
get up.

In Richmond, Yorkshire, ten of us spent the night in the
elastic home of David and Margaret Gray, who evicted their
children from their beds for us and tucked them away in

some corner—I never found out where. Margaret worked as an occupational therapist in a hospital for stroke patients. I told her about the book I was writing. She helped me to visualize Daphne.

Late on the evening of September twenty-second, we reached York, coming in at Bootham Bar two hundred years and a day after Woolman. The Mount School put up the women and Bootham the men. It was fun being in boarding school!

The following day, we visited Almery Garth, the house where Woolman was lovingly nursed by Esther and Sarah Tuke and where he died. In the afternoon, we walked on the city wall to Bishophill, the Friends Burial Ground. There, York Friends joined us for a Meeting for Worship under the lime tree and sycamore that shade Woolman's grave.

The only American there, I recalled that, thanks to Woolman, Friends in America renounced slavery a hundred years before the Emancipation Proclamation. Even before the Revolutionary War, no one who owned a slave could remain a member of the Society of Friends.

This Woolman Walk was not so much a commemoration of a death as the celebration of a life that continues to inspire us.

In York, we parted regretfully. We had shared a spiritual experience that made us, who hadn't known each other before, feel very close.

Andrew went to the station with me and got me into the right train.

Flying over the Atlantic, I remembered what Woolman wrote after his visit to Maryland Friends in 1766—that he "found peace in that I had been helped to walk in sincerity, according to the understanding and strength given me."

For me, this walk was an inspiration. When I got home, I

continued writing *I Take Thee, Serenity,* "according to the understanding and strength given me." I hoped I was being "helped to walk in sincerity."

But the quotation at the front of the book is not from Woolman. It is taken from Henry David Thoreau's *Walden:*

> Only that day dawns to which we are awake.

The book is dedicated to Ellen.

Living so intensely in an imaginary world, listening to the voices of paper people, I feared I was becoming disoriented until I had readers and found they could enter my world; that Firbank seemed nearly as real to them as it did to me.

Objective first readers, to whom one dare entrust one's manuscript in its fragile, unfinished state, are rare.

I was extremely fortunate. At various stages, Gordon and Edith performed this service, tenderly but candidly and competently. When I next went to England, I took the manuscript with me. Hugh and Shifa encouraged me, too. I could not have stayed the course without the assurance these four gave me that the world I described lived for them, too.

Tom and Katherine checked the book to make sure the flora and fauna of Firbank corresponded with that of the southern Rhode Island shore.

But my beloved critic, Henry Cadbury, was not, after all, among my first readers. Just before the book was finished, his wish that he not live to be "too old" was suddenly granted.

We who had turned to him for enlightenment and confirmation always came away with more than answers—a greater vision, greater openness to alternative views, a greater dedication to accuracy, in short, to Truth. We had been in touch with an almost Olympian clarity and sympathy, communicated, even at ninety, with boyish wit.

Wanting Henry's blessing, I hesitated to send my vulnerable characters out into the cold world. Would they evoke love?

I didn't have to wait long to find out. My literary agent soon informed me that the editor was delighted.

It wasn't until the contract was being discussed that I learned this book was going to be published as a juvenile, intended for young adults but not for older adults. I felt that the book might well appeal to teenagers but that it was about the meaning of marriage, which is not only the concern of children. So I asked the agent to withdraw the manuscript and offer it elsewhere.

She sat in her office on Madison Avenue and asked herself which editor in which publishing house would most appreciate *I Take Thee, Serenity,* finally deciding to try Ruth Hapgood at Houghton Mifflin in Boston. She didn't know Ruth and didn't know that Ruth and I were friends.

Ruth wrote back, "How nice of Daisy to ask to have her manuscript sent to me!" I, of course, didn't know anything about it.

Later, Ruth told me that she read the manuscript with tears running down her cheeks. When her worried secretary inquired what was the matter, she answered, sobbing, "It's this book."

Thus began one of my happiest experiences—working with Ruth.

Houghton Mifflin in Boston, Robert Hale in London, The Reader's Digest Condensed Books, Ballantine Books, and the Family Book Shelf brought Peter and Serenity and Oliver and Daphne into millions of homes and libraries. The Friendly Press of Waterford issued the book in Ireland.

A popular television producer wished to make the book into a two-hour film. If I relinquished the rights, I'd lose all control. Would the film be made in good taste? I felt responsible not only to myself but to Friends. During Yearly Meeting, I asked Mary Hoxie and Gordon and Tom Bodine to advise me.

After weighing the possibility of indelicate handling against the importance of the message in the novel, they agreed that I should take the risk. When I telephoned to New York to accept the offer, I learned that the young woman who was scheduled to direct the film and who might have done it sensitively had suddenly died. Her successor seemed to be indifferent to my feeling about the treatment. So I kept the rights.

The response to the book was beyond anything I envisaged. Masses of letters from unknown readers showed how hungry the world is for the Quaker way of life, at least on paper. I was urged to write a sequel. I didn't feel ready.

Douglas Steere, the much-loved Friend who is professor of philosophy emeritus at Haverford College and is known throughout the world as an interpreter of religious groups to one another, sent me this hilarious anecdote:

While I was on some recent journey, it was told me that in a certain Quaker meeting two of the members who were living together in a "stable relationship" finally decided to marry and asked the meeting for its permission. At the monthly meeting, which felt enormously relieved by this request, one of the male Friends was so touched that he rose and said, "Dear Friends, may we not give some little expression of how happy this request has made us by sending these dear Friends a copy of Daisy Newman's moving book, *I Take Thee, Chastity?*"

23

When *I Take Thee, Serenity* was finished, I wrote *On Turning Seventy.* Only a page long, it was addressed to myself.

If you're an artist with enough to live on and (overlooking a twinge or two) in fair health, it's a rewarding age. You've served your apprenticeship. There's no further need to compete, to prove yourself. The bliss of creating was always yours, yet now something new is stirring in you: a secret knowledge, an intimation, waiting to be revealed in your work. Why couldn't it have come sooner?

All those years had to be used up first, crammed with experience, joys, and sorrows . . .

These days, joy irradiates your spirit. . . . In a reversal of roles, the children have become your solicitous parents. . . . As for the grandchildren—! And all along the road, caring people have touched you with a bit of their greatness . . .

You're free now to pour out your whole essence, just as, at sugaring time in Vermont, you used to pour maple syrup over the family's pancakes. It took gallons of sap, piles of cordwood, and hours of boiling on the back of that superannuated stove to produce enough syrup for a single breakfast, yet you poured it with loving abandon—the whole distillation of your labors.

No, it won't last long. Nevertheless, it's a beautiful time, a time of value, even promise . . .

Ruth Osborne, who had become Ruth Woodbridge, asked me to write another pageant. Working with her before had been such a joy that I began *Peaceably with All Men,* based on the activities of New England Friends in 1775. Ruth produced it at Wheaton College during Yearly Meeting in 1975.

The British retaliated for the Boston Tea Party by closing the port, sending in troops, and making General Gage the governor of Massachusetts. Deprived of shipping, Boston was ruined. Food was scarce. Smallpox raged. Many people fled to the country without any means of support.

On the eighteenth of April, 1775, General Gage sent a force to Lexington and Concord. The next day, someone "fired the shot heard round the world." On July third, General Washington, sitting astride his horse under the elm in Cambridge, took command of the American army.

To Washington's headquarters in Craigie House, which later became the home of the poet Longfellow and which still stands on Brattle Street, directly opposite the Friends Center, came a delegation of three Friends, headed by Moses Brown of Providence. They brought a message from Rhode Island Friends announcing their intention to distribute relief to the sufferers in Boston "without distinction of sects or parties."

The three Friends asked for permission to enter the town. General Washington told them that no one was allowed to cross the lines.

Refugees were streaming north and so the Friends caught up with them and gave the food and money that had been intended for the sufferers in Boston to seven thousand "poor, necessitous persons" on the roads.

The title of this pageant is taken from a letter that Providence Friends wrote to "their beleaguered brethren in Boston," stating that the money was to be used for the relief of the besieged, "such poor, necessitous persons as are not Concerned in carrying on, or promoting Military Measures, without Regard to religious sects, or political parties . . . to live peaceably with all men."

The last pageant that Ruth and I would ever do together, it is dedicated:

To Henry Joel Cadbury, always our friend and mentor

That summer, I wrote a short story about a girl who comes home for Christmas vacation in her freshman year at college very much changed and feeling out of place with the people she loves. She goes to Kendal to pick up her grandfather and drive him to her house. The grandfather must have reminded me of Hugh, for when she arrives, he asks, "How is thee?"

Me? she thought. Miserable, but I can't tell Grandfather. I just said, "Me? I'm okay."

"In thyself? How is thee in thyself, Content?"

A magazine accepted the story, paying half on signing and promising to pay the other half on publication. But in September, when the story should have been going to press, the magazine informed the agency that it had received more advertising than it had expected and the story would not appear until the following Christmas.

The next year, the magazine asked that I delete the Quaker references and change the girl's name.

This was a Quaker Christmas story—something unique —and I didn't want to destroy it. So I asked the agency to withdraw the manuscript.

Later, I lengthened it into a novella and, having already been paid a good deal for it, gave it to Philadelphia Yearly Meeting, which published it very handsomely under the title of *The Wondrous Gift.* This is taken from Phillips Brooks's carol, "O Little Town of Bethlehem."

Throughout the week before Christmas, Bill Cavness, host of the program "Reading Aloud," read *The Wondrous*

Gift in installments over WGBH, Boston's Public Broadcasting station.

In November of 1975, my friend Thornton suddenly died.

I thought of his kindness to me, the pleasure of listening to his jovial conversation. I thought of the day he came down the hill and saw me working in my garden; how he stopped his car and got out—painfully, it seemed. But he bubbled over with happiness as he reached for a manila envelope that lay on the front seat.

"The last chapter," he announced, waving the envelope before my eyes. "And tomorrow I'm going to be seventy-six!" He was on the way to the post office with the last chapter of *Theophilus North*.

A few days later, I received a note:

What must you have thought of me!—dashing up to you like an urchin on his sixth birthday and showing you his new red shoes!

You must know well the feeling of having finished a work that's absorbed you and having nothing to do. . . . I've done my daily stint for so many years. . . . Writing is, among other things, a habit and I expect to be back in harness very soon.

But he wasn't. His health had declined.

Just before that last chapter, Theophilus North confides:

There were tears in my eyes. I am never so happy as when I'm inventing. . . . I said hesitantly, "I always find it hard to say good-bye."

I found it very hard to say good-by to Thornton.

Critics and scholars would, I was sure, be assessing his work and the impression he made on his public for decades. I wanted to share the way he was with his neighbors—

affectionate and unpretentious. Entitled "Remembering Thornton Wilder," the article appeared in *The New York Times* on the first anniversary of his death.

In it, I expressed the hope that the "House the Bridge (of San Luis Rey) Built" would some day be a national monument where Thornton's readers could go and "catch an echo-in-time of the voice we heard there." Imagine my joy when my friends Bob and Ellie Adair bought the house! After I moved away, they made me welcome in it whenever I came back to visit.

Houghton Mifflin had given me a contract for the book I was planning to write about Nannerl Mozart. I had told Bruce and Rosalind that it was going to be dedicated to them in gratitude for the joy their friendship and music had given me. But I hadn't even started to write.

I couldn't settle down. After *I Take Thee, Serenity* came out, I was asked to speak on the Sunday afternoon of Philadelphia Yearly Meeting. Westtown School invited me to give the Shoemaker Lecture, William Penn College asked me to come to Oskaloosa as writer-in-residence, and Pendle Hill announced a workshop entitled "Three Writers on Writing." The three were Elizabeth Vining, Mary Hoxie Jones, and I.

In preparing these talks, I was greatly influenced by Hugh Doncaster, who had a strong testimony against writing a speech in advance. He said he thought about it while he weeded his garden and when he couldn't sleep at night, but he refused to put it on paper lest he deliver it when he stood before his audience, even if he should suddenly feel that the group seemed to need something altogether different. A speech should be a response.

Being far less capable than Hugh and very insecure, I did write out what I prepared but I never consulted my notes when speaking. For I saw a parallel with vocal ministry in meeting—an address should arise as the common thoughts of those who are gathered together to seek light. It should not simply be my thoughts, composed when I was far from those to whom I was going to speak. I didn't want to give a speech; I wanted to hold a conversation.

All this occupied me. And my dear house—I was about to leave it.

On turning seventy, I had decided that I ought to be living nearer one of my children. I had looked at houses in Concord, Massachusetts. Nothing seemed just right. Then Kathy found the one in Lincoln that I'm living in now. It's only two miles from Wayland, where she and Nicky live. The place seemed made for me. But I wasn't able to move in for a year.

During that time, bills for real estate taxes and electricity were sent to my new address and forwarded to Connecticut.

Early in May of 1977, ten days before I moved, I went to Lincoln to make sure the painting had been done, stopping at the post office to ask that my mail be held, as I would soon be coming.

The clerk said—rather offhandedly, I thought, when I saw the postmark—"There's a letter for you here right now."

It had been lying there for two weeks!

I'm sure if the clerks had known that instead of a bill, this was a proposal of marriage, they would have been more solicitous.

24

The letter was from George Selleck, who was under the impression that I had already moved. He was asking me to consider marriage. His daughter Roberta was, he wrote, in accord with his proposal. It took me completely by surprise.

We'd known each other for over forty years. During twenty-eight of those years, George had been executive secretary of the Friends Meeting at Cambridge. When I was working at Radcliffe, we worshipped together there every Sunday. We both served on the American Friends Service Committee and the Cambridge Friends School board of trustees. George and Florence had stayed with me in Hamden and, when they went to live on Nantucket, after George retired, I often visited them there.

Like everyone who knew him, I held George in great affection and esteem, yet, like Loveday in *Indian Summer of the Heart,* I didn't feel that marrying again was in "right ordering," as Friends say, for me. My children agreed.

Just then, it was impossible to give something so momentous much thought, for I was getting ready to move.

When the dogwood blossoms were at their most splendid, I gave a farewell party to which I invited only those who had built the house and had laid out the garden. It was a significant gathering. These men and their wives had lived through a tense, creative time with me and had given my house and garden the same care they would have given their own.

The day I moved, after all the furniture had gone, Ted and Annette came, bringing lunch. They helped me to get the house in the condition in which I wanted to leave it. Knowing how sad I was, they stayed behind when I left and waved from the window so I wouldn't feel I was abandoning my dear house, leaving it empty.

After I got to Lincoln, I continued to believe that marriage was out of the question. I kept thinking up reasons.

At one point, I wrote to George, "I should have told you—I'm no cook."

He wrote back, "Do you think you can get me to withdraw my offer because you're no cook? *I* can cook."

When he came to visit me, I said, "I can't get married. I'm under contract to Houghton Mifflin for a biography."

George countered, "I'll help you. I'll take some of the housework off your hands."

What a dear man! How could I have held out so long?

How dear he was I began to realize during his visit. I was constantly surprised by the joy it was to have him around. My children, however, weren't going to let me go lightly. They urged me to take more time before coming to a decision.

Apart from the turmoil of my own heart, I was touched by the pathos of a man who has been faithful to one woman for more or less fifty years and, after long celibacy, falls in love. What does he know about the art of courtship, he who never looked at any woman but his wife? His very virtue renders him helpless.

George's habitual reserve, coupled with his need to share his life, moved me deeply.

I confided in Ruth, who had been my friend before she became my editor.

"I'm discovering," I told her with surprise, "that an old man in love is like a young man. Some day, when I get this troublesome biography off my hands, I'd like to write about that."

Ruth exclaimed—bless her heart!—"I hope you won't

let a little piece of paper stand in your way. If that's the book you want to write, forget the contract. Forget the Mozarts."

Forget the contract? Forget the Mozarts? Would that be right?

Ruth added, "You're talking about a sequel to *I Take Thee, Serenity.*"

Yes! This would be Oliver's book.

It was as if I'd been holding my breath all those years and now I could let it out! I could give up on Nannerl, although in the contract this new book would always be referred to by the title I had chosen for her biography.

I was ready now to write the sequel—more than ready. The story was all there, in my mind, eager to be written down.

Ever since Daphne died, halfway through *I Take Thee, Serenity,* Oliver had been lost. After nursing her so tenderly for years, he was adrift, even though Serenity and Peter were living at Firbank, making his home comfortable, and their little boy Ross was giving him great joy.

Suddenly, Oliver would fall in love.

What? Hadn't I vowed long ago that I would never try to write a novel seen through the eyes of a man? How could I be sure that what I described about his feeling was authentic?

How? Wasn't a real-live Oliver revealing this to me every day? All I had to do was look at George.

My friends urged me to open my mind and seriously consider marrying.

Even before I was able to do that rationally, my heart had taken George in. I still wasn't able to appreciate the extent of happiness that lay in store for me when I accepted his generous spirit, but I felt certain now that I was prepared to care for him in any eventuality.

George was not only winning me over. More and more, my children were coming to appreciate him. We soon had their wholehearted support and wrote to Friends Meeting at Cambridge, requesting marriage under its care.

Women were beginning to keep their names when they married. I told George I hoped it wouldn't hurt him but I wished to do that. I'm not a feminist. I just think a woman shouldn't be obliged to give up something so much a part of herself as her name, if she wishes to keep it.

George voiced no objection.

On the eighteenth of March, 1978, we were married in the Framingham Friends Meetinghouse.

Penelope, who saw to everything, had had extra benches brought in. The sun shining on the snow outside and the warm fire burning in the meetingroom gave the day a special radiance. On each windowsill, Molly had placed a vase with a single daisy, set off by red maple buds, foretelling the coming of spring. Ellen and Nancy played a Mozart duet at the back of the room, while George and I stood in the doorway.

When the music came to a close, we walked in and squeezed onto the bench by the fireplace with our children.

Margaret Welch, the Grossmanns, Jock Forbes, and the Walters served as the overseers of our wedding. Our family and friends, some of whom had come from New Haven, surrounded us with love. In the opening silence, several people spoke movingly. Myra's ministry touched me especially, for I knew how sick she was.

After George and I made our promises to each other, Nicky reached over and gave George the ring.

I held out my hand and had a shock. I was still wearing the old ring! George had intended to remove it in a little private ceremony before the wedding, but in our excitement, we both forgot. I tried to take the ring off quickly. After fifty years, it proved hard to dislodge.

Carol brought over the little table with the certificate. When we had both signed it, Roberta read it to the assembled guests who, being the witnesses, would sign it during the reception. Then Nancy and Jimmy carried out the table with the certificate and the Meeting for Worship continued until George and I brought it to a close.

Friends had prepared everything for the reception. It was beautiful.

A week after the wedding, we went to Hamden and stayed with Bruce and Rosalind. New Haven Friends gave us a second wedding reception. Annette had baked a cake, making it as nearly like the Framingham one as she could.

We went to see Walter and Myra, who had only met George at the wedding. The ease with which they accepted him made me very happy. Who wouldn't love George?

Then we flew to England. Tom Bodine met our plane and drove us to Woodbrooke College in Birmingham, where we had three interesting weeks, attending lectures. George gave one on Nantucket that was very successful. At the end of our stay in Woodbrooke, Tom drove us around to visit our friends in the North of England—the Doncasters, Elfrida, the Wilsons. At the end, we went to London and stayed with Millior Braithwaite.

Then we returned home. We had decided that we would live in my house during the winter and spend summers in George's. Early in June, we moved to Nantucket.

There, in the little upstairs bedroom that faces the garden, I began the book that became *Indian Summer of the Heart.* This is how the story opens:

In the summer of his seventy-ninth year, Oliver Otis of Firbank Farm fell in love, not circumspectly, as an elderly widower might properly do—to secure companionship and decent cooking—but wildly, without design, head over heels.

The preposterous situation frightened Oliver. It was unseemly.

At thy age! he reproached himself a dozen times a day.

He could think of little else . . .

I'm ordinarily calm, Oliver argued with himself. All my life, my emotions have been pretty dependable. How did they get so out of control? . . .

He told no one, naturally.

At times, he suspected that Serenity and Peter Holland, who lived with him, had a tiny inkling. They seemed to regard him more tenderly these days, almost in sorrow, as if they feared that his judgment was impaired.

For their sake, Oliver thought . . . I ought to explain; assure them that I'm not senile, only in love.

"What shall we name the woman Oliver's in love with?" I asked George.

He answered without hesitation, "Loveday."

I thought he was referring to Loveday Hambly, the "Quaker Saint of Cornwall," who visited Fox when he was in prison in 1656, but it was to someone more recent. George explained that during the Friends World Conference, held at Oxford in 1952, which we both attended, he had met an English Friend named Loveday Selleck and ever since he'd been intrigued by the name. That is how the object of Oliver's affection came to be called Loveday.

Once named, she turned into a real paper person and I began to see that this wasn't going to be only Oliver's story. It was Loveday's, too. Parts of the book could only be related through her. And so the points of view began to alternate. The opening section is seen through Oliver's eyes, the second one through Loveday's. Part Three would be Oliver's again; Part Four, Loveday's. Then Oliver would have the last word. In that way, we would come to know Loveday's personality at firsthand.

She is completely different from Oliver in taste and background, coming as she does from a section of the country far removed from New England.

Again I was influenced by George. Loveday would be from Emporia, Kansas, where he was born. The fact that I had never been to Kansas gave me pause, for I depend on the description of the landscape my characters are rooted in to convey their moods. But I wanted to bring Emporia into the story.

Just the place-name seems to have cast a spell, at least for one unknown reader. When the book appeared, I had a letter that began:

> I'm from Kansas and thoroughly enjoyed your *Indian Summer of the Heart.* Had I not been from Kansas, I know I would have enjoyed it anyway.

Although Loveday appears to be self-sufficient, she betrays a secret longing for Oliver's way of life. But she has her own intellectual interest. It should be in a field he knows nothing about, such as music. This would give her something of value to bring to him.

Nannerl Mozart! Loveday would write her biography. That would absolve me from my obligation! There wouldn't be room for all the material I had collected, but I'd use the best.

When we returned to Lincoln, I got up very early and did some work while George was still asleep. As each chapter was finished, he read it aloud to me so I could hear whether the sound of the words was pleasing. From the first, he saw himself in Oliver.

Certainly, his goodness and beautiful spirit are there. But the fact is that the character I call Oliver was realized before George became the center of my life. Honesty demanded that I tell him.

"Well," George argued persuasively, "Oliver and I are the same age and the circumstances are the same."

As time went on, I saw him in the book more and more. But I hated to shut myself up to write, instead of being with him.

My children took him into the family with all their hearts. My grandchildren became his, the only ones he had. My Harvard house made him an affiliate, too. We took an active part in Friends Meeting at Cambridge. Most of all, we enjoyed being at home together.

Each day was a festival for me.

25

On our first anniversary, our children, grandchildren, and friends came to rejoice with us.

Three days later, George suffered a stroke. When he woke up, after being comatose a long time, he couldn't speak. What I had made up in *I Take Thee, Serenity* turned out to be prophetic.

I was in Oliver's place now, caring for George as Oliver had cared for Daphne.

For sixteen months, George was helpless—sad, testing months, yet also glorious, in the way that love makes shared suffering glorious. We soon learned to communicate. To the end, George remained the same person, gracious and accepting.

When the nurses failed us, the children and grandchildren flew to the rescue. Our friends supported us. Andy and Merrilie came almost every day. During Yearly Meeting, Ted and Annette came from Hamden to take care of George so I could attend some of the sessions. I only stayed long enough to hear an inspiring talk on the Old Testament given by Moses Bailey, our witty and self-effacing nonagenarian, who had been George's teacher at the Hartford Seminary and whose friendship meant a great deal to us both.

The Steeres and their daughter Anne came to the hospital Christmas Eve. Christmas Day, Ben and Laura came with their little girl. Wendy, who had edited George's book, chose to celebrate her thirty-sixth birthday there with him.

Every First Day, a little group of Friends arrived to worship with us, wherever we happened to be, at home or in the hospital. And while George couldn't say so, he let us know how much this meant to him. In the strange state in which he suddenly found himself, the familiar Quaker silence assured him that he was still the person he had always been.

He was such a modest man that he had never been able to appreciate the extent of his service. When he became executive secretary of the Friends Meeting at Cambridge in 1936, there were eleven members. The meetinghouse had not yet been built. When George retired in 1964, there were over three hundred members and so many attenders that it was necessary to hold two Meetings for Worship of a Sunday. George's concept of Quakerism as an inclusive mode of worship, his care for each individual, transcended differences. People of every belief felt, as they joined in the silence, that they had come home. This universality was proclaimed in George's whole manner. He did indeed answer "that of God in every one."

During his illness, when his friends expressed love and gratitude for the help he had been to them on their spiritual journey, George may have realized for the first time how much he had done with his life.

After a year, he began to speak a little. One First Day in Cambridge, this miracle took place, to the joy of all who heard his voice again.

A few weeks before he died, his great nephew, Ron Selleck, came with his wife and baby. They supported me during that difficult time. Linda relieved me of the housekeeping and little Sarah refreshed my spirit each evening when I came home from the hospital.

George died on the eleventh of July, 1980.

In the Meeting of Thanksgiving for his life, many spoke of the insight he had given them. I thought of William Penn's "short epitaph" to George Fox. It applied equally to my George: "Many sons have done virtuously in this day, but, dear George, thou excellest them all."

The Memorial recorded by New England Yearly Meeting recalled that when George and Florence retired to Nantucket in 1967, bitter young people were coming to the Island in droves. They "found themselves listened to with respect, worshipped with, and wisely ministered to by this rather dignified and formal-looking but remarkably open-minded and caring couple."

Friends Meeting at Cambridge received contributions in George's memory from many people who had left the area and wished to signify how much his influence continued to mean to them. After a time, the Meeting decided to use these gifts and part of the fund that had been donated for expansion of the Friends Center to create a George Selleck Room in it.

An unused sleeping porch opening off the executive secretary's office was transformed by Chris, a devoted attender and a skillful architect, into a beautiful room. One has the impression that it is actually built into the trees, for there are branches at all but one of the many windows. The soft colors of the walls and carpeting give a sense of restfulness.

Molly, our master woodworker, made the exquisite tables in the Selleck Room. On the large drop leaf we placed the copy of *Quakers in Boston* that had been lovingly bound by Larch. Over the table we put a picture of George, smiling at us in his outreaching way. The small table between the corner windows, made of walnut with a maple inset, is the gift of Nantucket Friends.

We had shelves built in an alcove on which to place the books from George's library. Sandi, the Friend who helped care for him in his illness, went over to Nantucket and brought the books back to Cambridge.

The whole room speaks of George in the peace and harmony that it communicates from the moment one opens the door. It is a much-needed refuge from the liveliness of the busy Center. Here one may come to read or meditate or hold a quiet conversation. Nothing, I believe, would have made George quite so happy as this tribute to the service he gave the meeting and the friendship he extended to all.

During the Meeting for Worship in which we dedicated the room, we became aware of the great number of people who contributed to its making. The architect reminded us that, no matter how beautiful a space may be, it is the use to which it is put that determines its character and she hoped we would endow the Selleck Room with the spirit we wished it to have.

A month after George died, when I had just gone back to *Indian Summer of the Heart,* I broke my hip at Yearly Meeting. My editor must have despaired of my ever finishing that book.

When I left the hospital, Nicky and Kathy took me to their house. There David Freudberg interviewed me for his National Public Radio program, "Kindred Spirits." As soon as I was able to sit at the typewriter, I started working on the book again.

The fitting title eluded me until one day, when I was looking through the works of John Greenleaf Whittier and came upon this in "Memories":

> Years have passed on, and left their trace . . .
> Yet hath thy spirit left on me
>   An impress Time has worn not out . . .
>   The shadows melt and fall apart,
> And, smiling through them, round us lies
> The warm light of our morning skies—
>   The Indian Summer of the heart!

Without George to serve as my living model, I worried again about my ability to write convincingly from a man's point of view. I asked Gordon to be on the lookout for any passage in the book that did not sound authentic. His vigilance reassured me.

The dedication had become evident. When I began the biography of Nannerl Mozart, which this book was replacing, I told Bruce and Rosalind that it would be dedicated to them. But George had not yet come into my life. By now, this book was his, as well. And so the dedication reads:

In memory of George Selleck
And for Bruce and Rosalind Simonds

Writing those last chapters would be hard, I feared. But, no. It turned out to be a solace. George was right there with me, continuing to live in the book.

And when Houghton Mifflin, the Family Bookshelf, the Reader's Digest Condensed Books, and Large Type Reader published it, people as far away as Italy and Australia found him there, too, in all his goodness, wisdom, and disarming simplicity. They wrote, great numbers of them, telling me how they had come to love him.

Isn't that miraculous? George and the other Friends who inspired me in the course of fifty years are still publishing Truth, entrusting their message to paper people. Philip Ludlow, Dilly Fuller, Serenity and Peter, Oliver and Daphne and Loveday, even little Ross and the dogs are carrying that message to millions of readers.

It makes me think of what Romain Rolland wrote:

Tout ce qui a touché à l'amour est sauvé de la mort.
All that has touched love is delivered from death.

26

Early in May of 1982, when I had finished proofreading *Indian Summer of the Heart,* Ellen and I flew to Norway to visit Nicky, Kathy, and Carol.

Ellen is so busy, teaching in the Case Western Reserve Medical School, heading the Liaison Service at the Wade Park Veterans Hospital, and consulting in the Children's Rehabilitation Hospital, as well as seeing private patients, gardening, and getting in trim for long-distance biking, that it was years since I'd had the joy of spending so many days with her.

Nicky was finishing the academic year as a visiting professor in Trondheim, not far from the Arctic Circle. He and Kathy didn't fly over. They crossed the Atlantic with three adventuresome companions in their thirty-eight-foot sloop *Katrina,* which, apart from the hull and deck, Nicky had built himself in his backyard in Wayland.

The previous June, Jimmy and I and a few friends had stood on the dock in Woods Hole, waving good-bye. Someone had brought a bottle of champagne. Before it could be uncorked, Nicky pushed off, leaving us to drink to *Katrina's* safe voyage while she motored away and was soon out of sight.

The transatlantic crossing called for all Nicky's skill and judgment, as well as Kathy's catering ability—provisioning for four hard-working seamen and herself. There had to be sufficient food to last three weeks, should the voyage take that long. And the drinking water was limited. Just stowing everything in the tight space—seventeen dozen eggs alone —was a challenge, to say nothing of cooking in a heavy sea, when Kathy stood at the gimbaled stove with a strap around her so she wouldn't lose her footing.

That transatlantic crossing demanded something of me, too—fortitude. While waiting for news of *Katrina's* arrival, I realized that my fear of some mishap on the ocean, tempered with faith in Nicky's seamanship, was a magnified version of the ambiguity I feel when I begin a book—fear that my ability may not be equal to my vision, alternating with faith that I shall be given the required strength.

Two weeks after she left Woods Hole, *Katrina* reached Oban in the Hebrides. What a relief when we at home heard that the voyagers had landed, safe and well! The two companions flew home and reported that Kathy's cooking aboard was as good as it is ashore. High praise!

After cruising in the Hebrides and Shetlands, where Kathy put in a supply of knitting wool as well as food, she and Nicky and a new crew sailed up the coast of Norway to Trondheim. There they found a house for the school year. Carol joined them at the end of August and was immediately taken into the cathedral choir.

When the Norwegian winter set in, *Katrina* was put up in a Trondheim boatyard. At last, spring arrived. So did Ellen and I.

The next day was my seventy-eighth birthday. It was not overlooked. But the big event was the launching of *Katrina*. Ellen and I stood on shore, watching her slide into the canal. Then the mast was stepped with less difficulty than I have threading a needle.

Too soon, the visit ended. Ellen and I took Carol with us to explore the fjords on the coastal express, the little steamer coming from the North Cape. Now it was Nicky and Kathy's turn to stand on the dock and wave. For two days we sailed among glaciers, rocky islands covered with birds, and fishing villages. We spent three days in Bergen exploring the town and feasting on smoked salmon in the open air. Then we parted, Carol to return to Trondheim, Ellen to fly home, and I to go to England.

Shortly before my eightieth birthday, I spent four days in Greensboro, North Carolina, as a "Visiting Friend" at First Friends Meeting. I also met with the Quaker students at Guilford College and the residents of Friends Homes.

This gave me a chance to visit the Moores, whom I hadn't seen in many years. Floyd had just retired after teaching Bible and Quakerism at Guilford. He was interested in my interpretation of Friends in the Kendal novels. His enthusiasm and affectionate praise would make the most undeserving feel successful. Lucretia's outpouring of love is expressed with flowers. They grace every room in her house. They even accompanied me when I left.

Speaking in public drains me, not alone because I'm trying to remember what I intended to say. While I'm speaking, I'm continually observing my listeners, hoping to see a response in their faces—concurrence or disagreement, no matter which—some evidence that I'm not delivering a speech but taking part in a spirited conversation.

Still, I left Greensboro refreshed by the warmth of my audiences and the joy of being with the Moores.

Shortly after my birthday, Mary Hoxie travelled all the way from Kendal in Pennsylvania to Providence, Rhode Island, in order to introduce me at the Conference of Quaker Historians and Archivists, where I'd also been invited to speak. Mary's gracious introduction and this celebration of a friendship that went back forty years touched me.

"Paper People: Publishing Truth in Fiction," I called the talk, in which I told how I came to be a writer and reviewed the circumstances that produced particular books. To these

Publishers and Caretakers of Truth, I ventured to suggest that a religion of experience, such as Quakerism, may best be communicated in fiction.

Once that talk was over, I yielded to the "motion of love" that had made me resolve to record for my children and grandchildren what I had told various audiences, but I would write more informally. Since this was not to be for publication, I could include more personal recollections.

In July, Patricia Wild and I went to Pendle Hill, the Quaker Study Center in Wallingford, Pennsylvania, to lead a writers' workshop. While we were there, Rebecca Mays, the editor of the Pendle Hill Pamphlets, asked me what I was working on. I told her that I had just begun to write about my literary experiences, stressing that this wasn't for publication.

To my surprise, Rebecca seemed very interested. She asked me to let her see the manuscript when it was finished.

I tried to make her understand that this was to be only for my family, but Rebecca repeated her request so persuasively that I promised to send her a copy when the account was finished, even though I knew that something so colloquial and intimate would have no place among the scholarly Pendle Hill Pamphlets.

After I got home, I continued to type my recollections. As I wrote about my childhood and my fitful education, I began to see a pattern emerge. Over and over, what had seemed to be misfortune at one stage of my life turned out to have been for the best. What had seemed to be an irrelevant occurrence proved to be part of a recognizable design.

At the beginning of September, I went to Woods Hole to see Jimmy. I told him that I was finding it harder as an octogenarian to keep house, nourish myself, see my friends, serve on Quaker committees, and also do a full day's writing.

Jimmy said, "Come down to the lab with me. Bring a page of your manuscript."

I couldn't imagine what he had in mind, but I was interested in going to the Oceanographic Institute and seeing where he worked. When we got there, he told his boss that he was going to show me a word processor. That's why he brought me!

He and his father had been trying for four years to persuade me to get one. I was convinced that I couldn't learn how to use it, that it wouldn't lend itself to my method of composing.

Jimmy seated me before a keyboard and told me to copy my page as if I were at a typewriter. I made some errors. He reached over and pressed a key or two. The errors were corrected like magic. But my typing wasn't appearing on paper, only on a screen. What good was that? Jimmy went off and returned with a beautifully printed page.

It was so easy! I was impressed. I was, in fact, hooked.

When Nicky came home from Norway, I told him that I had decided to buy a word processor. He couldn't believe it. In half an hour, his son had accomplished what he'd been unable to do in four years.

As an affiliate of North House, I was entitled to a very large discount at the Harvard Computer Store. But the model I wanted—the one Nicky had—couldn't be delivered for several months. Having taken four years to make up my mind, wouldn't you think I might have waited another few months, I who am usually so thrifty?

That weekend I said to Nicky—it must have been a leading—"Now is when I need it. If I can get it right away, I'll pay the full price."

Monday evening, Nicky came in with boxes and boxes,

which he took up to my room. He had to saw off the feet of the table to make it the right height. Electrical cords lay everywhere. Did I really want all this stuff?

For the next four days, Nicky and Kathy spent every spare moment teaching me how to use the thing. When they weren't here, I'd call them up for help. But I was beginning to catch on.

Seven chapters of *A Golden String*, covering only the first twenty years of my life, when I hadn't yet published, were already typed. I started to put them on the computer. Late Friday night, I'd only copied five, but I fell into bed.

At four in the morning—it was the autumnal equinox—I woke up. My left arm and leg were tingling. The sensation was so mild, I wasn't worried. I didn't know that this was only the prelude.

I went to the kitchen and made coffee. Then I sat by the phone, waiting for Nicky and Kathy to wake up. At seven, I dialed. I said to Kathy, "I think I've had a stroke."

She asked, "Have you called the doctor?"

I said, "No. I don't want to wake him this early."

She said, "You'd better call now."

Dr. Keevil—"Dr. Liveek" in *Indian Summer of the Heart*—came at once. I begged him not to put me in the hospital. He told me to stay quiet for the next few days. He'd keep an eye on me.

Nicky and Kathy intended to go to Woods Hole for the weekend. Afraid they'd change their plans if I stayed alone, I asked one of George's nurses to come for the day. My friend Bar phoned. When she heard what had happened, she said she and her dog were coming to spend the night. I protested. They came.

I fell asleep early. Near midnight, I woke up and got out of bed. After I'd taken a few steps, the floor suddenly opened under my feet. I couldn't have reached the phone to call for help. I held on to the furniture and shouted for Bar. By being there, she saved my life.

When I turned eighty, I vaguely expected some disability to develop—a minor inconvenience. Now, only three months later, I was in the hospital, unable to move my arm or leg. *That* I hadn't bargained for! Compared to George, though, I was lucky. I could speak.

For years, I had been working on forgiveness—forgiving those who had hurt me, forgiving my own shortcomings. All that first week, I kept telling myself that I had to forgive this cerebrovascular accident, too. I mustn't waste what little strength I had on anger. In this hospital bed, I must begin to put my life back together. If I could just bear my stroke with a little of the grace with which George bore his—

Ellen arrived and conferred with the doctors. She and Kathy thought it would please me if they were to put my last two chapters on the computer. They had trouble deciphering my notes. This mark of their love touched me. But what good were those chapters now? I'd never be able to finish the book. My writing days were over.

After weeks in the hospital, I came home. Nicky and Kathy and another of George's nurses were waiting for me. They had prepared the downstairs bedroom and moved the bench out of the entrance hall so I could get around in George's wheelchair, which stood by the door, ready to receive me. As I was lifted into it, I burst into tears. I was so happy to be home!

Nurses around the clock—the expense was frightening. Why had I rushed to buy that computer and printer? I'd never use them again.

Two months later, I had a second stroke, this one thalamic—sensory. My muscles worked but the brain wasn't getting messages through to my limbs. None of the medication relieved the pain, which grew worse every day, till it seemed unbearable.

My friends held on tightly to the part of me they had always known, the part that the pain obscured from my own vision. It was their tenacity and my children's patient endurance through all my complaining that finally pulled me through. Bar, Rosly, the Towls, the Grossmanns, Patricia and Wendy, Penelope, and all the others who reassured me that behind my body's agony there was still the person they had always loved—it was thanks to them and to the neurologist whom I eventually consulted that I returned to my former self.

At Christmas, I had nothing for anyone. I asked Nicky to get my seven chapters copied for the family and a few friends. Thinking of the book I had envisaged and looking at the thin volumes that served as my meager gifts that Christmas, I felt sad. As promised, one went to Rebecca at Pendle Hill.

A few months later, Rebecca telephoned. Did she have my permission to present my chapters to her publication committee? There were enough pages for a pamphlet.

I told her to do as she wished but I knew those chapters weren't suitable for a Pendle Hill Pamphlet.

My ball of golden string had rolled away. I'd never retrieve it.

Afterword

Over the years, I had given some manuscripts to Guilford College and the galleries of *Indian Summer of the Heart* to Haverford. After my talk to the Quaker Historians and Archivists, Edwin Bronner, librarian of Haverford College, asked me to deposit George's and my papers in the College's Quaker Collection.

The manuscript of George's book was already there. Going through his letters and notes made me sad. The Grossmanns helped me to deal with them.

My own papers were a mess. I didn't know what I had and couldn't climb upstairs to look in the files.

My friend Charlotte Tinker, who had recently retired after serving as secretary of the Wider Quaker Fellowship and a member of the publications committee of Philadelphia Yearly Meeting, came and spent a week carrying down masses of stuff. Reviews that had been stuck away in bundles she spread out and pasted, one by one, in the scrapbook my mother gave me. She sorted piles of letters from friends and unknown readers who wrote about the books. I hadn't realized how many people cared. But I did appreciate what Charlotte did. It took me months to go through all those papers.

Our friends surrounded me with the loving attention they had given George. Rosly and Penelope came Sunday after Sunday to worship with me. So did Nancy and Bill. One afternoon, while Mary-Frances, a friend from Pennsylvania, was visiting me, a night nurse arrived who announced that she was coming down with a bug. Mary-Frances sent her away and stayed with me till morning.

Nicky put up a metal bar so I could practice walking. He built a ramp with a railing that made it possible for me to go out on the terrace. Ellen phoned every few days and listened to my complaints, which she discussed with one of her most respected colleagues in the hope of getting help for me. She thought that if I could just start to write again, I might forget the pain for a while. So Nicky brought the computer down and put it in the living room.

At the end of April, a neurologist I consulted prescribed the medication that quieted the pain I had endured, not very bravely, for months. I could even walk a little with crutches. No one had to hold on to me any more! Energy I had needed to fight pain was released for more pleasant activities, though I still had very little endurance.

Jean, my English daughter-in-affection, came. I was so glad to see her! Now in her middle fifties, Jean is a literary woman, too, the editor of a newspaper-on-tape for the blind.

Iola Cadwallader, a Friend living in Iowa, wrote to ask whether she might make a musical of *I Take Thee, Serenity*. She proposed to write the libretto, the music, and the lyrics all herself. What a delightful prospect!

One day, Rebecca called from Pendle Hill to tell me that her committee didn't think those chapters were suitable for a pamphlet.

Just what I'd said all along!

But, Rebecca went on, the committee would like me to finish the book I'd begun. I must, however, have in mind a wider audience than my family. Many people would read the book. Pendle Hill wished to publish it.

Pendle Hill was retrieving my golden string!

I told Rebecca that there was a risk. At my age and in my condition, I might not be able to finish, but I hoped I could.

My left hand was too weak to write or type accurately.

The word processor! If I hadn't acquired it before I was stricken, I never would have. Getting it when I did was truly a leading.

Looking through the papers Charlotte had brought down, I discovered notes for speeches I'd given over the past forty years, letters from editors and fans, and reminders of events long forgotten. When the box of manuscripts and letters finally stood by the front door, waiting to be picked up and shipped to Haverford, it weighed thirty-two pounds.

The letters I had received from Thornton I gave to Yale.

Memories those papers stirred excited me. New chapters of *A Golden String* began to evolve. Writing had always led me in at heaven's gate. Now it assured me that, slowed up though I was, I could still do my work.

While Pendle Hill was preparing to issue a limited first edition, the ball of golden string rolled westward, clear to the Golden Gate. There John Shopp, an editor at Harper & Row, San Francisco, picked it up, and he and his firm decided to publish a much larger edition. Then the ball rolled eastward again and Mary Risley of the Family Bookshelf, which had offered *I Take Thee, Serenity, Indian Summer of the Heart,* and *Diligence in Love* to its members, also selected *A Golden String.*

Where are we now?

Well, Ellen's snow peas are coming up. Irv is back from Japan, where he lectured to medical colleagues on the *corpus luteum.* He's translating Dutch books into English. He and Ellen are getting in trim for biking from Cleveland to Woods Hole in September. At the rate of fifty miles a day, it should take them three weeks.

Nicky and Kathy are once more aboard *Katrina,* somewhere off the coast of France, en route to Portugal. There they will leave the boat and fly home so Nicky can do a little work at M.I.T. to support *Katrina,* as well as the rest of his family. Kathy will go back to her job at the Wayland Library until November, when she and Nicky will return to Portugal to sail *Katrina* to the West Indies. There they will leave her again and work till next summer. Then they will sail her from the West Indies to Woods Hole, her home port.

Jimmy is leaving for Scotland in a few days. He is coauthor of a paper that will be presented at a conference in Aberdeen. He's still working at the Oceanographic Institute, doing the programming for the little unmanned submarine that is being built. It will explore the ocean floor at great depths.

Nancy has finished her second year in medical school. That makes her half a doctor! She is about to go to Toronto for the summer conference of the Young Friends of North America.

Carol has just graduated from Connecticut College. She has a job rigging sailboats. Later, she'll sign on as a member of *Katrina's* crew.

And I? Mostly, I'm trying not to worry about those sailors who are heading for the Bay of Biscay. And I'm working hard to learn to walk a little better.

A month ago, I turned eighty-two and Eleanor, who at six inspired my first stories, celebrated her seventieth birthday. Last week, I was the speaker at the sixtieth reunion dinner of my Radcliffe class, which considers me an alumna, even though I was only there one year. I was also invited to the twenty-fifth reunion dinner of the class that came to live in Holmes as freshmen the first year I was head resident. It made me happy to know that those women looked back fondly on our time together.

Everyone is most kind about taking me around. Yesterday, Rosly took me to Meeting for Worship in Cambridge. In the afternoon, Ruth took me to Framingham to have tea with her mother. Tonight Rosly will take me to Cambridge for a meeting of the advisory committee and tomorrow the Towls will take me there for a working session of the oral history project. We are trying to assemble a body of interviews with older members of the meeting. I love going to that working session because it takes place in the George Selleck Room.

This afternoon I was asked to write a pamphlet for the Friends General Conference on marriage. Is that what I'm meant to do next?

Gratitude for the love and support given me throughout my life, which I felt so deeply on my eightieth birthday, overwhelms me now. Without the care I received during the past year and a half, the efforts of so many people, I would never have recovered enough to write this.

It may well be my last book. And yet, I still feel the promise I felt when I turned seventy, the intimation waiting to be revealed.

Again I wish that I could name each one who contributed so generously to my life. That isn't possible. But this book, originating as a "motion of love" for my children, has reached out to embrace all of you.

Wherefore, seeing we also are compassed about with so great a cloud of witnesses, let us lay aside every weight . . .

CHRISTIAN HERALD ASSOCIATION AND ITS MINISTRIES

CHRISTIAN HERALD ASSOCIATION, founded in 1878, publishes The Christian Herald Magazine, one of the leading interdenominational religious monthlies in America. Through its wide circulation, it brings inspiring articles and the latest news of religious developments to many families. From the magazine's pages came the initiative for CHRISTIAN HERALD CHILDREN and THE BOWERY MISSION, two individually supported not-for-profit corporations.

CHRISTIAN HERALD CHILDREN, established in 1894, is the name for a unique and dynamic ministry to disadvantaged children, offering hope and opportunities which would not otherwise be available for reasons of poverty and neglect. The goal is to develop each child's potential and to demonstrate Christian compassion and understanding to children in need.

Mont Lawn is a permanent camp located in Bushkill, Pennsylvania. It is the focal point of a ministry which provides a healthful "vacation with a purpose" to children who without it would be confined to the streets of the city. Up to 1000 children between the age of 7 and 11 come to Mont Lawn each year.

Christian Herald Children maintains year-round contact with children by means of a *City Youth Ministry.* Central to its philosophy is the belief that only through sustained relationships and demonstrated concern can individual lives be truly enriched. Special emphasis is on individual guidance, spiritual and family counseling and tutoring. This follow-up ministry to inner-city children culminates for many in financial assistance toward higher education and career counseling.

THE BOWERY MISSION, located at 227 Bowery, New York City, has since 1879 been reaching out to the lost men on the Bowery, offering them what could be their last chance to rebuild their lives. Every man is fed, clothed and ministered to. Countless numbers have entered the 90-day residential rehabilitation program at the Bowery Mission. A concentrated ministry of counseling, medical care, nutrition therapy, Bible study and Gospel services awakens a man to spiritual renewal within himself.

These ministries are supported solely by the voluntary contributions of individuals and by legacies and bequests. Contributions are tax deductible. Checks should be made out either to CHRISTIAN HERALD CHILDREN or to THE BOWERY MISSION.

Administrative Office: 40 Overlook Drive, Chappaqua, New York 10514
Telephone: (914) 769-9000